THE BEST OF DICK IDOL'S WHITETAIL WORLD

Hunting The Four Periods Of The Rut

THE BEST OF DICK IDOL'S WHITETAIL WORLD

Hunting The Four Periods Of The Rut

by Dick Idol

Bigfork, Montana

Dedication

To my wife, Robin, who has graciously learned to live with my all-encompassing lifestyle of hunting and outdoor activities.

To my mother, Peggy Idol, who has always supported me and encouraged me to follow the less-traveled path.

To my dad, who early in life introduced me to the world of hunting and fishing.

To my two sons, Cody and Colt, who hopefully will have many years ahead to enjoy the wonders and pleasures of the outdoor world as I have done.

To Carson Smith, who has been a friend and hunting buddy through thick and thin.

And finally, to my deceased uncle, Ed Cheek, who regularly took me deer hunting before I was old enough to drive.

Table Of Contents

SECTION III — LAYING THE FOUNDATION FOR PATTERNING

SECTION IV — THE FOUR PERIODS OF THE RUT

Acknowledgements

THIS BOOK REPRESENTS MORE THAN ONE MAN'S OPINION on whitetail hunting. It is in fact a window into my life and very soul. Whitetails and whitetail hunting have been my pleasure, sport, career, livelihood and purpose in life. To me, whitetails and my being are inseparable. And, I have certainly not arrived at this point alone!

There have been many throughout the decades who have been friends, supporters and contributors in helping me get to where I find myself today. To all those, I owe a special gratitude and great deal of thanks. The list is too extensive to cover everyone in this limited space, and I apologize to those not mentioned. But here, I would like to extend special thanks to:

• David Morris, who not only has been a longtime friend, hunting partner and business collaborator but also is the individual primarily responsible for the publication of this book.

• Steve Vaughn, Chuck Larsen and other staff at Game & Fish Publications, who have always been supportive, patient and willing to cooperate in the many whitetail projects we've shared over the years.

• Gordon Whittington, who has always provided editorial inspiration, guidance and technical direction, in addition to being a friend, hunting partner and principal contributor to making this book a reality.

• Jim and Dick Cabela, Dennis Highby, Pat Snyder, Gregg Severinson and many others at Cabela's, who have always been supportive, enthusiastic and cooperative in our many joint projects.

• The many individuals and companies in the outdoor/hunting industry that have allowed me to have a part in their endeavors, such as Jim Crumley, Trebark; Ronnie Strickland, Mossey Oak; Lock-On Treestands; XI; NRA; Dixie Deer Classic staff; Tom Murchison, Arkansas Big Buck Classic; Hugh Price, Minnesota Deer Classic; Jerry Johnston, Texas Trophy Hunters; and many others.

• My hunting buddies — Carson Smith, Danny Allen, Kirk Sharp, Charles Stone, Derrick Graham, Scott Taylor, Tim Condict, Guy Shanks, John Brekke, Jim Shockey, Darwon Stoneman, C.J. Abatel, Rick Blase, Jim Bevins, Tommy Baine, Frank Boling, Jerry Ippilito and last but not least my brother, W.C. Idol, who was guiding and hunting with me when still wet behind the ears.

• The many successful big buck hunters who kindly took the time for interviews and photographs for stories.

• Finally, those individuals who have shared my special interest in big bucks — Fred Goodwin, Widmere Smith, Phillip Schlegel, Charles (Chuck) Arnold, Larry Huffman, Brad Gsell, Gale Sup, Walter Schreiner, C.L. Gage, Jr., Gary Machen, McLean Bowman, Dave Boland, Randy Bean, Gary Donald, Mike Gillis, Scott Lennard and Phil Soucy.

Editor's Note

by Gordon Whittington

A S EDITOR OF *NORTH AMERICAN WHITETAIL,* the magazine express-
ly devoted to serious trophy whitetail hunters, I've seen "deer
experts" come and I've seen 'em go. They often appear out of thin
air, write a few articles and star in a video or two, endorse a line of
products and voila, they've arrived. A few years later, though, most
are as hard to find as a Boone and Crockett buck, having disappeared from the scene with the same suddenness that marked their
arrival.

But Dick Idol, the whitetail expert who wrote the book you're
about to read, doesn't fit that mold.

What's different about the man from Montana? Good question,
and one not all that simple to answer. I've spent more than a decade
trying to figure it out myself, and I'm not sure I have it all in a neat
little bundle just yet. But as the only person to have edited Dick's
magazine articles since the fall of 1984, during which time he's written roughly 500,000 words about big whitetails, I suppose I'm as qualified as anybody else to take a stab at it.

Part of Dick's secret of longevity in this business, I believe, is
the fact that he's one of us. Like so many other members of the hunting public, he grew up in a rural environment and learned to love
deer and other wildlife at an early age. He wasn't exactly born with a
silver grunt call in his mouth, either, so his early days of whitetail
hunting were spent in much the same way as ours were — hunting

close to home with family and friends. Even though Dick has since hunted whitetails all over North America, his formative years in North Carolina have served him well and he has not forgotten who deer hunters are and what they really want out of the sport. He's been there.

But, a lot of the so-called "experts" started out as ordinary hunters. How did Dick get so far ahead ... and stay there? Mainly through an intense personal desire to go and do and learn, starting long before trophy whitetail hunting was the rage it is today. He was into all sorts of specialized whitetail activities, from shed hunting to trophy outfitting to putting on shows, before most hunters ever figured out that bucks lose their antlers each year. Dick was never one to let other folks push the envelope.

Having said that, I also must admit that he was a bit slow to get into a certain whitetail activity, and ironically, it's the one for which he has ultimately become best known. You might figure that somebody who was well ahead of his time in so many areas would be eager to break new ground in writing about trophy whitetails as well, but he honestly wasn't.

Back in '83, when *WHITETAIL* magazine was itself little more than a newborn fawn, Dick was serving as its Research Director, and David Morris, who was editor then, decided that maybe he should be writing, too. He balked, saying, "I've never written anything."

Finally, the guy was coaxed into giving it a shot ... and the rest, as they say, is history.

I wish I could take credit for launching his writing career, but I didn't come aboard as editor until about a year later. By then, Dick already had the hang of converting his knowledge into the printed word. And as a result, readers from one end of North America to the other were finding out there really was more to trophy hunting than they'd ever thought. Dick had just raised the bar to new heights.

In the years since then, much has happened on the whitetail scene. Many "wannabes" have come and gone, while Dick has continued to present his insights on big bucks to an eager audience. And oh, by the way, the number of folks interested in those insights has continued to soar, reaching a level few observers could have imagined even 15 years ago.

Coincidence? I think not.

Foreword

by David Morris

I FINALLY HAD TO ASK, "Who the heck is Dick Idol?"
The first annual Dixie Deer Classic was only four or five hours old, and already I'd heard his name mentioned at least a dozen times. I knew he was one of the speakers, as was I, but beyond that, I knew nothing of the guy — except that a lot of hunters in his hometown of Raleigh, North Carolina, thought Dick Idol was deer hunting's cat's meow.

The fellow to whom I asked my question looked surprised then stated matter-of-factly, "Why, Dick is one of the best deer hunters in these parts, and he's really into big whitetails."

To this day, I'm not sure I've ever heard a more apt description of Dick Idol. He is indeed one of the best deer hunters in these parts, only nowadays, "these parts" has expanded to include all of North America. And though it was back in March of 1982 that I first heard the words, "he's really into big whitetails," now, nearly 15 years later, those words are hardly adequate to express the fervor with which Dick Idol is "into big whitetails."

My first chance to get to know Dick came when my host and good friend, Carroll Mann, gathered the speakers for dinner on the opening night of that first Dixie Deer Classic. The talk naturally turned to whitetails and whitetail hunting, and it didn't take long to realize that this Dick Idol I had heard so much about was in a league of his own when it came to big whitetails. He not only knew how to hunt them, but he had made a study of big bucks — actually, giant bucks — having delved into, among other things, where the biggest bucks in the world had come from and who had killed them and how. Plus, this guy had collected newspaper clippings, magazine articles, amazing photos — lots of them — and, yes, even the antlers of giant bucks from across North America. Dick Idol was indeed into big whitetails!

By the time that night was over, Dick and I were fast friends. At that time, Dick was planning to use some of the photos and antlers he had collected as part of the displays in a national whitetail and taxidermy show he was organizing. Since I was in the publishing business, I was more interested in the possibility of getting some of those incredible photos and monster racks onto the pages of a magazine. I returned to Game & Fish Publications offices in Georgia with a sample of Dick's photos. Upon showing them to my partner, Steve Vaughn, he immediately had the same interest.

Within a day or two, Steve and I were on an airplane to Montana, Dick's recently adopted home, to meet with Dick and discuss his role and the use of his material in a whitetail-only magazine. The rest is, as it were, history. The first issue of North American *WHITETAIL* magazine came out in October of 1982, with Dick serving as the research editor, a job for which he was uniquely suited.

Since then, nearly 200 Dick Idol articles, more than any other writer, have graced the pages of *WHITETAIL* magazine. Dick's reputation as a top whitetail hunter has now spread far beyond the Raleigh area to every place whitetails are pursued. Having chased bucks across North America with Dick, I can honestly say he is one of the finest hunters I have ever shared a camp with. He not only hunts with intensity, purpose and determination, but when Dick steps into the woods, he becomes a predator, moving fluidly and silently through the shadows. Couple this natural talent with practiced skills, a great knowledge of the whitetail and an intense desire to successfully challenge the biggest of the breed, and you have a whitetail hunter par excellence. Best of all, Dick knows how to impart his knowledge and experiences through the written word, which he does here in this book.

Speaking of this book, the topic, "Hunting The Four Periods

Of The Rut," is a subject Dick is uniquely qualified to write about. After all, he set the pace for patterning bucks and for dividing the fall into distinct periods based on movement patterns in his landmark *WHITETAIL* series in 1990 entitled "Patterning Bucks Throughout The Season." Dick is probably best known for his extensive writings on buck travel patterns and how to apply them to hunting one particular buck. That vast store of knowledge is all brought together here in this book.

Dick's whitetail involvement is not limited to just his writings. In recent years, Dick has presented lectures and seminars at virtually every major outdoor show in the U.S., including the N.R.A.'s Hunters Tour and Whitetail Super Clinics, which he helped originate. He has made celebrity appearances in stores and catalogs such as Cabela's, L.L. Bean and Bass Pro Shops. Dick has collected and exhibited racks and sheds from the world's most legendary bucks and has produced many whitetail products, including five major videos. Most recently, he has received wide acclaim for his whitetail sculptures and drawings. His first major sculpture, Midnight Crossing, a quarter-life-size bronze of a big northern buck, is considered by many to be the finest whitetail bronze on the market.

Today, it wouldn't surprise me to hear someone say that Dick Idol is "one of the best whitetail hunters in these parts" or that "he's really into big whitetails." What would surprise me, however, would be to hear someone say, as I once did, "Who the heck is Dick Idol?"

Introduction

by Dick Idol

THE "EVOLUTION" OF A BIG BUCK HUNTER is quite a remarkable phenomenon and journey. How do hundreds of thousands of serious trophy whitetail hunters "grow up" to be so similar when there are no institutions, corporations or organizations promoting the cause? Why does one brother become a whitetail fanatic while the other only hunts one weekend a year?

To my knowledge, there is no grooming of promising individuals to become big buck hunters nor is the carrot of fame or economic gain dangled to entice would-be participants. There are no rules, guidelines, standards or measures that describe the "politically correct" conduct or perspective for a big buck hunter, yet there is great uniformity and a common mentality among all in this vast group. Even when two total strangers who happen to share a passion for big buck hunting bump into each other at a movie, the post office or wherever, they can, upon broaching the subject of whitetails, strike up a conversation spoken in big buck jargon that would make a bystander presume they were first cousins.

I don't know all the "whys", nor do I really care. I'm just glad it's so. I happen to be one who falls into this group of committed whitetail fanatics. Big whitetails have had a profound affect on my life. To state it more directly, except for my family, whitetails and whitetail hunting are and have long been the most important thing in my life! And, I am by no means alone!

I suppose I evolved into a big buck hunter in much the same way as thousands of others. My first exposure to deer hunting came through family and friends. And, I took to it like a hereford calf to a milk bottle. At first, I was excited when I just found deer tracks. Then came a deer in the flesh — a doe. And finally, the ultimate — a whitetail buck. When I actually shot my first buck, a small 5-pointer (eastern count), I'd reached the big time!

Early in this evolutionary process, I ran the gamut of big game — from polar bears in Alaska to elephants in Africa — but the white-tail kept drawing me back and gaining in priority. Through old books, taxidermy catalogs, and hunting magazines, I became ever-more fascinated with legendary big bucks and whitetail hunting. Big whitetails were in my blood; there was no denying it. The passion was, in fact, so strong that whitetails and hunting became a part of my career early on. But being only a part wasn't enough — ultimately, whitetails became my life. My whitetail career has been and still is a wonderful journey that hopefully will continue for years to come.

As I worked my way up the ladder to bigger and bigger bucks over the years, my standards moved ever higher and I eventually set about to hunt some of the biggest bucks in North America. Yes, one of the great side benefits of my career has been the wonderful opportunity to hunt many of the best big buck regions of the world. (My wife, Robin, thinks hunting is my career and that everything else revolves around it. Even if she's right, I won't admit to it.) Wherever I've hunted them, big bucks are the same — reclusive, nocturnal and evasive. They are the ultimate survivor in the world of big game.

As I started hunting the oldest and wisest of the whitetail clan, I was forced to develop a certain mind-set and hunting strategy that would give me the best odds of success. I had to come up with a more planned, methodical approach that would reduce my dependence on the luck factor and give me more control over the outcome of the hunt. I had to get to know the animal well enough that I could predict what he was going to do, even before he did it, at different times of the year, in different types of habitat and under various conditions and circumstances. The process was slow, but in time, I began to unravel the mysterious world of the big buck.

During my whitetail journey, I've learned a tremendous amount about big whitetails, though my learning curve is still on the climb. My burning desire to learn as much as possible about them stems from my goal to kill truly big bucks, no matter where they happen to live. This is no small feat, as evidenced by the minuscule percentage of the more than 13 million whitetail hunters who have never killed a true trophy whitetail. The fact is that big bucks anywhere are tough to successfully hunt. I believe they offer the ultimate hunting challenge, which accounts for their incredible popularity.

Since 1982, I have regularly written articles in *North American WHITETAIL* magazine. These articles have chronicled my progress and education — my evolution, if you will — as a big buck hunter. During the years of learning, I have developed new approaches and strategies and refined old ones as better ways became evident. For a long time now, I have written about such concepts as hunting individual bucks, understanding and predicting buck behavior and travel patterns, hunting the four periods of the rut and of course, applying the right hunting tactic at the right time and in the right way. These articles have come at different points along my learning curve, and in magazine articles, only small portions of the big picture can be presented at one time.

Well, this book is an effort to bring together in one place my most current thinking regarding what I've learned and written about over the last 15 years. Obviously, I can't cover everything even in a book, but this volume represents my most up-to-date perspective on many aspects and components of hunting big bucks. Hopefully, you will find that this rather complex subject is represented in an understandable and logical way.

Even after you read this book, there obviously will be more to learn. Big bucks will still come out on top more often than not. But most will agree, the challenges, the pursuit, the learning, the game — that's what the hunt is all about.

THE BEST OF DICK IDOL'S WHITETAIL WORLD

Hunting The Four Periods Of The Rut

by Dick Idol

THE GAME PLAN

Chapter 1

Laying Out A Strategy

THERE ARE MANY WHO SIMPLY GO HUNTING and let the chips fall where they may. There's certainly nothing wrong with this approach as long as the individual is satisfied with the results. But for me, and I suspect most of you reading this book, I want to increase my odds as much as possible. Since we can do little about the luck factor, we must focus on those aspects we can influence. That means developing a strategy.

In trying to get a handle on the big picture strategy, I divide the overall game plan into three distinctly different components. They are:

1) Locating the best area to hunt then finding a specific buck within that area.

2) Understanding and predicting the buck's travel patterns.

3) Applying the best hunting tactics.

LOCATING THE PLACE AND THE BUCK

Locating The Place To Hunt

The general region and specific area we ultimately choose to hunt has everything to do with our success. For some fortunate hunters, a trip to Canada, Texas, the Northwest, etc. may be in order. Others may seek out better trophy territory in neighboring states or perhaps one of the better areas in his home state. Some hunters can find big bucks close to home, but even then, exactly where they choose to spend their time — the best farm, lease, ranch, etc. —

This massive Alberta non-typical, with 6 3/4-inch bases and a "caribou-like" freak shovel, was taken by the author because he knew the buck was in the immediate area. On the fifth day of hunting him and after a variety of tactics, success was finally realized by forcing the deer to move on a two-man drive. Photo by Kirk Sharp.

goes a long way toward determining the outcome of their season. The point is that it's critical to invest your time where your chances of success are best. Nothing is more important than this. Make the best choice possible given your time and resources.

Obviously, putting ourselves in the best places and determining overall buck quality require lots of effort, research, homework and time. One rule of thumb to get a quick handle on the likely buck quality of an area is the amount of hunting pressure. The higher the pressure, the poorer the trophy potential, and vice versa. So, look for areas with the least amount of hunting pressure. There, you'll generally find more big bucks, and they'll be easier to hunt.

Finding A Big Buck To Hunt

The second part of the "locating" component is finding a specific buck to hunt. The idea is this: Success will be higher when we are spending our valuable hunting time in the vicinity of a previously located buck that meets our size standards. It's difficult to kill a

Richard Pauli's wide 267 3/8 Illinois non-typical was taken after hunting the buck for three consecutive seasons, during which time he saw the buck several times. By concentrating his hunting time in the buck's known area, he was finally successful. Such extensive time and effort spent on a known deer dramatically points out how unlikely it is to kill a buck like this by accident. Photo by author.

150-class animal, assuming that's your target size, when hunting an area where bucks of that size are practically non-existent. This is especially true in the case of exceptional bucks. The larger the buck, the fewer of them in the general population and the less likely it will be that such a buck is in the immediate area you're hunting.

"Big" is, of course, relative to the region. A 140-class buck may be common in Saskatchewan but extremely rare in Louisiana. If a 165-class buck is the goal, even in Saskatchewan bucks of that size aren't everywhere so substantial scouting and homework must be done to be sure such an animal exists where you're hunting. In setting standards, remember: As the size standard increases, the number of bucks meeting that standard decreases and they become progressively more difficult to hunt. The biggest bucks are the rarest and the toughest. So if your standard is set high relative to the area, it's vital to have a particular buck located to maximize your odds. We can spend our time looking for a buck to hunt or we can spend our time hunting a buck we know is there. That's the choice.

UNDERSTANDING HIS TRAVEL PATTERNS

Once we have chosen a region to hunt and have located a specific buck, we need the advantage of understanding how he lives and moves throughout his range. To attempt to hunt a big buck without a general understanding of his behavior and travel patterns is little more than bumping around in the dark hoping for a lucky encounter. To me, a true understanding of travel patterns and all the related elements affecting those patterns is the most important key to figuring out the whitetail ... and to big buck success. The bulk of this book will be devoted to shedding light on this vital subject. Once these fundamental concepts and understandings are in place, choices of where, when and how to hunt become more obvious.

APPLYING THE HUNTING TACTICS

With our hunting area selected, a specific buck located and knowledge of his travel pattern as complete as possible, we are ready to hunt the buck. As you will see later in the book in several of the graphic illustrations outlining hypothetical travel patterns, there are many possible locations where a buck may be hunted and numerous choices of tactics to capitalize on the vulnerable points of his travel pattern. We will discuss some of these options as we look at travel patterns, but we will delve into the best tactics in detail in Section VI.

As you can see, all these components of the game plan are interrelated and each is an important part of an approach to increase the statistical odds of shooting a big buck. The chapters to follow are intended to lay a foundation of understanding so that common sense and logic may be applied to make sound hunting decisions.

LOCATING A BIG BUCK

Chapter 2

Hunting Where
The Big Bucks Live

O<small>VER THE LAST</small> 25 <small>YEARS,</small> I'<small>VE WATCHED WHITETAIL HUNTING</small> grow in many directions. Despite what we sometimes hear about hunting being in trouble, there are more avid participants today than ever before. Hunters overall are more knowledgeable and sophisticated in their tactics, and as an industry, the sport has matured to a certain degree. Through it all, there has always been the common thread of big bucks.

We're sometimes told that meat was considered to be the only thing worth bringing home from the deer woods in "the old days," but the earliest whitetail hunters were infatuated with impressive antlers. Hunters today are even more so. Even the most devoted self-described "meat hunter" generally will take a big buck when given the choice between tender venison and a big rack. So, I think it's fair to assume that most of you are interested in hunting big bucks, as opposed to simply trying to fill a tag with just any deer.

It's apparent to me that when it comes to locating and hunting trophy bucks, our skill level most often will determine our success rate. And to be sure, skill is a package deal far more comprehensive than simply knowing how to shoot or being well versed in woodsmanship. Hunting big bucks successfully demands that we not only have knowledge but also the right attitude — a willingness to put forth the effort to be consistently successful.

I realize that a great percentage of you do have an above average commitment to your whitetail hunting; otherwise, you wouldn't even be reading this book. But, I'd like to point out that what I'm

If your sights are set on a big buck like this one, time and effort are required to be sure such an animal lives where you hunt. You can't kill what's not there. Photo by Neal & Mary Jane Mishler.

advocating is not necessarily for everyone. Each of us should feel comfortable in getting what we want from the sport of deer hunting. I'm certainly not saying that every individual who takes to the woods should be committed to harvesting only big bucks. That's a personal choice based on many factors, such as available time, other hobbies or simply one's own ambitions. Having fun is the bottom line. But for those who seriously want to be more successful at consistently taking big bucks, extra effort and a higher level of commitment are parts of the overall package that will lead to positive results.

Central Saskatchewan is justifiably famous for its giant whitetails. This 200-class typical was shot on an Indian reservation in the Battleford region of Saskatchewan in 1993. Photo by author.

Playing the percentages

Our effectiveness at locating and hunting big bucks can be gauged on a sliding scale. To be successful in bagging every trophy we pursue would result in a perfect score of 100, while never bagging a big deer would give us a score of 0. Frankly, we won't ever reach the top level on this scale, but we want to do what we can to approach such consistent success. This, in essence, is what becoming a more accomplished trophy hunter is all about.

The "luck" factor always will have a significant influence on our results. But, there's a fine line between where luck leaves off and the results of our own actions take over. That line can be moved upward on the scale — we can "make our own luck," as the old saying goes. This is especially true when the object is big bucks.

In this effort to make our own luck, one of the most fundamental elements, in my opinion, is the necessity of hunting a known, individual buck. But believe me, even this is absolutely no guarantee of success. Ten to 15 years ago, I was under the naive delusion that I could kill virtually any big buck I went after, given enough time and the right conditions. Wrong! In several cases over the years, I went after specific big bucks and quickly learned the taste of humble pie, in quite large quantities I might add. As I set my mind on becoming better at the difficult task of hunting top-end deer, I soon realized that these monsters always keep the odds of survival in their favor, no matter how skilled the hunter pursuing them might be.

I feel the most optimistic odds of consistently taking a particular buck are no better than one out of four, or 25 percent. Those odds can be even worse when other hunters are added to the same patch of woods or when unhuntable private land lies within the buck's home range. These and a myriad of other factors can increase the difficulty of taking a big buck. When such problems arise, the chances of your bagging that deer could drop to 20 percent or lower.

While those odds might not seem very high, as I look back over my whitetail career and all of the big bucks I've hunted during that time, I'd be happy to have taken my 20 percent! What's really pointed out by this "statistic" is the difficulty of taking a particular big buck, even when the plan is sound and the effort serious. And if these animals are so hard to harvest when hunting them purposely, no wonder they routinely avoid hunters who simply hope to bump into them at random.

Not surprisingly, then, one of the most important elements of successful trophy hunting is the task of locating an individual buck that meets the standards of the hunter. Without such an advantage, I think the chances of consistent success drop nearer to one percent, or lower. It doesn't take a rocket scientist to compare 1-in-5 odds with 1-in-100 and see the value of knowing that a prime buck is in the area being hunted.

Is he really there?

The fact is that most people hunt an area and hope there's a big buck in the vicinity. We all tend to be creatures of habit and take the path of least resistance. It's just easier to hunt the old lease we've

The Midwest, with its fertile soils, nutritious food sources and great genetics, is turning out some of the biggest bucks in the U.S. This book-class whitetail was photographed there by Bill Kinney.

been on for five years or an uncle's place where we don't even have to call ahead for permission. But many times, there's not a big buck living on such properties. That convenient spot simply might not be the best place to spend our limited days afield.

If you look at the pure odds built into a hunting season, often it's easy to see why certain hunters are far more successful than others. For example, if you can only hunt weekends for two months during the season, that translates into just 16 to 20 days of actual hunting. If many of these days are spent looking for a buck to hunt, obviously the odds of success are not nearly as good as they would be with all 16 to 20 days being spent in the range or vicinity of a known trophy buck. That principle holds true whether you hunt one day or 100 — the odds are always better when your time is spent in an area containing a big buck!

While some hunters spend much of their valuable hunting time searching for an animal to hunt, others spend hunting time in areas that don't hold a single deer meeting their standards. It's been said many times before, but you can't kill him if he ain't there! If you're looking for a buck that will score at least 150 Boone and Crockett points but there's not one in the area you're hunting, I can guarantee that you won't kill one. It's such a basic premise that retelling it here hardly seems appropriate, yet I see it happening all the time across North America.

Just as some hunters restrict their efforts to a convenient area, others hunt strictly according to buck sign. But again, the mere presence of buck sign doesn't guarantee the presence of a big buck. Fresh rubs and scrapes certainly indicate the presence of at least one buck in the area, but in most cases, determining precise antler quality from such sign is a long shot at best. Of all the variables involving buck sign, the diameter of the trees being rubbed and the amount and type of damage done to them most accurately reflect overall antler size, but even this is far from an exact science. There is certainly a distinct difference in the characteristics of rubbing damage done by a 110-point buck versus a 150-class deer, but there might not be a great deal of difference between the sign left by a 140-class animal versus that of a 175-class record buck. The most useful scenario is to first locate the buck and then use such sign to specifically define his travel pattern.

What's "big?"

Frequently, I use the term "big buck" without really defining it. To me, "big" is relative. Obviously, when I'm hunting the Hill Country of Texas or the sandhills of Florida, my own definition of what's "big" changes from what I would consider "big" in Alberta. (If it didn't, there would be little point in my ever hunting an area with smaller deer — unless I didn't care to shoot anything there.) First and foremost, the term "big" is directly relative to the area being hunted, and it can change when the same hunter goes to a different area. It happens all the time. For example, when a hunter from an area with few mature deer goes on a guided hunt in Canada, almost automatically the hunter's minimum standard of what represents a "shooter" buck goes up from what it would be in his home area.

"Big" also varies from hunter to hunter based on his experience, personal hunting goals, time available for hunting, etc. The typical progression normally begins with a novice hunter being happy to take a few bucks of any size, then holding out for bigger animals as he gains experience and the novelty of just filling a tag wears thin. The minimum standard for a particular hunter with a bow also might be lower than for the same individual in firearms season. Regardless of whether your standard is a 150-class buck or simply any buck that's above average for the area being hunted, the discussions and theories provided throughout this book will apply.

The biggest are the toughest

Anyone "unfortunate" enough to have that insatiable appetite for big bucks and the willingness to do something about it might as well resign himself to the fact that it's a tougher row to hoe. Built-in deterrents exist before we even start. In the first place, hunting the biggest bucks in any given range almost automatically means we're after a relatively small percentage of the deer in the herd. In heavily pressured areas, only one percent of the population might be outstanding bucks. In fact, in certain out-of-balance herds, the percentage could be even lower. There simply aren't many of what we're looking for out there.

This relatively small group or bucks we're after also happens to be the target of a lot of other hunters. Not only can this cause a reduction in the number of high-quality bucks available, but it also

In 1918, John Breen shot this incredible 202-point typical in Minnesota. Considered by many to be one of the greatest typical whitetails ever killed, this buck is the fulfillment of every deer hunter's dream. Photo by author.

results in another major problem for the trophy hunter — nocturnal animals.

Of all the unique qualities of the whitetail, perhaps the most impressive is his ability to pattern and react to humans. He has been smart enough to figure out that, overall, danger is lowest at night. Consequently, he has learned to be as nocturnal as necessary to survive. This is his greatest asset and the hunter's worst handicap. And, the particular segment of the deer population we're primarily interested in happens to be the most nocturnal of all. Throw in the fact that even those big bucks that do move in daylight generally stick to heavy cover and remote areas, making them less visible than other deer in the herd, and it's easy to understand the mature whitetail buck's reputation for being the world's greatest hunting challenge.

Not only are big bucks more difficult to hunt, but to be successful in taking them consistently, serious time and effort are required to locate and pattern them, particularly in the off-season. More work is required to find prime hunting areas and to get access. But for those who have known the satisfaction of walking up and grabbing a heavy beam, the extra effort, days of frustration and passing of smaller bucks are definitely worthwhile.

It's been said that if a buck makes it through 4 1/2 years in a moderately to heavily hunted area, he's virtually unkillable. I certainly understand why the saying evolved, and I would agree that bagging such a deer is generally a difficult task. But, many big bucks are killed all over North America each season and not all of them are taken simply as a result of "lucky" encounters. Through knowledge and smart hunting choices, we can drastically improve our odds on the big ones.

Chapter 3

Zeroing In On An Individual Buck

BEFORE I GET INTO THE SUBJECT OF THIS CHAPTER, I want to briefly discuss my approach to scouting — something that is vital to both finding a big buck and to figuring out his travel patterns.

Our discussion of scouting here will be very brief, because as you will see, this aspect of hunting will be incorporated into much of what we will be looking at in the following chapters and the "how-tos" of it will become clear. I break scouting into two parts — primary scouting (general) and secondary scouting (specific) — although if I'm actually hunting, both can be underway at the same time.

Primary scouting gives us the "must knows" about the range of our buck. This includes critical geographical features such as cover (or lack of it), fields, fencelines, lakes, bottlenecks, hills, swamps, etc. Such features as road systems, access points, parking areas, walkable trails, edges and powerlines will influence the pattern of hunting pressure and consequently where and how deer move. All these elements combine to give us a good idea of the playing field upon which we're about to engage our buck.

Now, secondary scouting. When the basic geographical features and general elements impacting travel patterns are known, specific movement patterns must be figured out just prior to hunting. Bedding areas, food sources, travel corridors, rut areas, doe concentrations, trail systems and security cover are all things we need to get a handle on. Sooner or later, we've got to decide exactly where and how we're going to hunt. This requires on-site ground work. The latest information gathered during secondary scouting will direct our

The author located this 180-class non-typical before the Oklahoma season begun and managed to kill him on opening day. It does not always work out that way, but hunting a known big buck is one of the real keys to being "lucky." Photo by David Morris.

immediate actions and point us toward what we hope to be the best tactic for the circumstances.

Locating a "shooter" buck

When I go into a new area to look for a big buck to hunt, my first move is to assess the amount and distribution of local hunting pressure. Big bucks do not live uniformly over a broad area but exist in pockets, largely because of the influence of this pressure. We can safely wager that, as a rule, the biggest bucks will not be found where the hunting pressure is heaviest.

In my scouting, I look at where most of the hunting pressure exists and then search for those out-of-the-way places other hunters tend to avoid or overlook for various reasons. A big buck often exists in a particular spot not so much because it has more productive habitat but simply because he wasn't shot at 1 1/2 or 2 1/2 years of age.

41

During the summer and early fall, the best place to start the search for a buck to hunt when season rolls around is at major food sources. This big 8-pointer is feeding in a pea field in August. Photo by author.

Thus, the availability of older bucks in one location versus another is largely a function of local pressure patterns. So as a general rule, I try to avoid the "hunting hotspots," as they are locally known. My goal is to find lightly pressured areas.

There are numerous ways to know if a big buck resides in your hunting area, though some are certainly more reliable and definitive than others. Obviously, seeing him with your own eyes or finding both shed antlers is best. But, there are several other possible sources of information, such as a reliable landowner or buddy (one who doesn't lie about such things), photos, etc., that could indicate the presence of a big one. Of course, I'll be the first to say that seeing the buck or coming up with other information to prove he's there is no small task.

The process of learning the whereabouts of a particular buck is greatly affected by the time of year in which the search is initiated. Say, for example, you first spot a big buck during the post-rut period when he jumps across the road while riding along just after deer season. Knowing you would like to hunt the deer, you immediately set about getting permission to hunt the farms in the area. This would potentially allow you to scout for the buck during the post-season, certainly one of the best times of year to decipher the buck's travel pattern and yet not worry about disturbing him. There's no other time of year when such a total accumulation of tracks, trails, rubs, scrapes, bedding areas and sign in general is present for study.

Unfortunately, bucks don't begin making rubs in earnest until mid-September, and scrapes appear in October or November, depending upon the region. Thus, scouting to locate and pattern the buck in hunting season means there's only a narrow window of time available in which to figure out what he's doing. Of course, the risk of disturbing him so close to the time for hunting is high. This can cause him to move out or become even more nocturnal.

Another plus for post-season scouting is the possibility of finding one or both of his shed antlers. On mature bucks, there is certainly no other evidence that shows us so precisely his rack characteristics. Like many other aspects of whitetail hunting, finding sheds is a skill that can improve with experience and overall deer knowledge. Most hunters find few sheds because they only look in the fall, when many antlers have been almost entirely chewed up by rodents and/or are hidden under grass or leaves.

In northern wilderness areas, bucks tend to shed their racks a lot earlier than do those in farmland areas, which I suspect is because of the relative lack of quality feed and the rigors of winter in the big woods. In most areas of the Northwest, Canada and even parts of the Northeast, antlers begin dropping in late December, with the majority falling off in January. In the richer farmbelts, many bucks carry their antlers well into February, with some even dropping in late March. The best time to find sheds is immediately after they drop or, in the case of snow country, just after the snow melts.

Probably one of the most overlooked scouting periods of the year is the summer, when most people have their minds on fishing, softball, vacations, etc. I feel sure there is no other time in which the big bucks are so visible. Beginning in May, bucks are growing their racks, a process which requires large quantities of high-protein foods. They also are putting on their winter fat supply. Generally

Rubs are the most useful sign for locating and patterning a big buck during the early fall. The velvet has dried on this buck's antlers, and he is about to start the velvet-shedding process. Rubbing will soon begin in earnest. Photo by author.

unmolested by hunters, they become very visible in the fields or around other high-quality food sources.

Normally, I consider July 4 the date when developing main beams have turned forward and a rack can be sized up as to its potential and overall characteristics. By the first week in August, the rack is fully formed, except for a small percentage of tine length. Velvet is usually shed during the first 10 days of September.

Bucks tend to be very visible in the heaviest growth stages of June and July, and they begin showing themselves less and less as August progresses. So, I normally concentrate my scouting, or "looking" as it's better described, from the last week in June through the second week of August. The summer months offer the added bonus of possibly seeing several bucks at a time, because those in similar age classes tend to reside in bachelor groups then. This behavior is part of nature's design to establish dominance ranking by nonlethal means. I have on special occasions seen as many as 8 or 10 big bucks feeding in the same field, though it's more common to spot only two or three together.

As fall progresses, bucks tend to abandon the "open" food sources and become more reclusive, often shifting to in-cover feed, such as acorns, nearer to their bedding area. The author refers to the time when that shift occurs as the "disappearing period." Photo by Roman Jaskolski.

In farm country, I try to establish the preferred food source, whether it's soybeans, alfalfa, peas or other high-protein legumes, and learn where these fields are located. Then, I check for tracks and either sit and watch (primarily in late afternoon) or ride/walk to check several fields during the last couple of hours of the afternoon. Normally, I use strong binoculars or a spotting scope to study racks, both for their potential and any distinguishing characteristics that would aid in future identification of a specific buck.

When the buck-location process begins in the fall, say late August or September, we have a whole new set of circumstances to deal with. In most regions, bachelor groups begin breaking up in late August and older bucks start coming to the fields later each day. Finally, many quit using the open feeding areas altogether in daylight. This often coincides with the maturation of the annual acorn crop in the woods, and deer enter what I call the "disappearing period." Now, they tend to drift back to their core area (unless the pre-

One of the best indicators of a big buck's presence in the area is his shed antlers. Look for them as soon as possible after they are dropped, which occurs in most places in January or February. Here, W.C. Idol (author's brother) is about to pick up a whopper Montana shed. Photo by author.

ferred food source was already in the core area) and travel very short distances between bedding and feeding sites. Big bucks are extremely difficult to locate visually during this time frame. Consequently, September and much of October are not great times in which to see big bucks from a scouting/locating perspective.

If you find yourself still hoping to locate a big buck during the fall, then sign-reading is the next-best bet. Specifically, rubs and rub lines are our best references for both locating and predicting travel patterns. As indicated earlier, this is not a perfect science. We might even get onto the wrong buck. But generally, rubs on "big" trees — say, two to six inches in diameter or whatever is "big" for rubs in the area being hunted — are about the most reliable sign we can trace back to the largest buck(s) present. Scrapes certainly reveal the presence of at least one buck, but they don't really separate out the big ones.

Although it's no easy task to precisely pinpoint a nocturnal and generally elusive big buck, the process of locating him, understanding his travel patterns, figuring out where he holes up in security cover and understanding how he survives in general is a great part of the hunt itself. To embark on the task of hunting an individual buck, especially a mature one, is to begin understanding why so many great whitetails die of old age.

Normally, if I'm going to be hunting in a particular area for several days, I like to have more than one good buck located. It's always possible that the first buck could be killed by someone else, and I want to at least have a Plan B to fall back on. Occasionally, if both bucks are comparable, I might hunt back and forth between them.

Hunting pressure

Our chances of success on an individual buck are greatly influenced by several factors. As we've discussed, the most dramatic of these is the amount of pressure being applied by other hunters. This primarily affects how nocturnal the deer will be during hunting season, and consequently, the degree of difficulty in patterning and seeing him. When possible, I try to not only locate an individual big buck to hunt but also to find one that offers the best possible odds. Obviously, hunting a 150-class buck on a heavily pressured public wildlife management area will offer much worse odds of success than will the pursuit of a similar buck located on a private farm only you are hunting.

The access issue

The degree of access to a particular buck's range will greatly influence your chances of success as well. When I refer to a buck's "range," I mean his "home range," the entire area he will travel at various times during the year, including the rut. In contrast, his "core area" is a much smaller area "imprinted" on him at a young age. ("Imprinted" is a biological term representing a strong instinctive attachment to a place or thing.) His core area is the heart of "where a buck lives." Depending on the buck:doe ratio and overall deer density, his range could easily span a two or three-mile radius, and it would not be unusual for his overall travel distance to be 10 to 15 miles! So, if you can only access 10 percent of a particular buck's range in one case but can hunt nearly all of another buck's range, you obviously will have much more favorable odds of success in the latter case.

I am especially careful about pursuing any big buck that lives along the edge of an unhuntable refuge or other large block of posted cover. In such cases, I'll normally suspect that his security cover — the place where he'll spend a lot of his daylight hours during hunting season — is off-limits to me. I try to avoid these bucks if I have other options.

Put time on your side

The amount of time we have to hunt also should have a bearing on which buck(s) we choose to pursue. There's not much point in trying to take on a tough case if we have only one weekend of the year to hunt. On the other hand, if we have the entire season to pursue a particularly challenging buck, the odds might be worth the gamble. Still, for most hunters in most situations, the smartest approach is to focus on whichever acceptable buck can be hunted the most and the easiest.

Certainly, our options on which bucks to hunt, the sizes of bucks we have to choose from and the various degrees of difficulty of taking any of them change from season to season. Common sense would tell us to hunt the biggest bucks that offer the best odds of success. If we do this consistently, we'll reap our rewards in the long run.

LAYING THE FOUNDATION FOR PATTERNING

Chapter 4

Understanding And Predicting Travel Patterns

ANYTIME WE GO DEER HUNTING, we are assuming something about travel patterns. When a treestand is put up, the site is not selected because the tree is pretty. Dog hunters don't turn the hounds loose in the middle of a 1000-acre field. Most hunters don't watch the fields in the middle of the day. And, deer drives aren't staged in woods where the hunters think there are no deer.

Regardless of the hunting method, any hunter worth his salt will give at least some consideration to where and how the deer are moving, when activity will occur and which areas are likely to hold deer at a given time. Even though they might not give it much formal thought, most hunters still factor likely deer movement patterns into their game plan. Here, we're going to focus on the importance of a thorough understanding of buck travel patterns, which essentially is how, when, where and why a buck travels over his entire range throughout the fall. Included in this will be his feeding and bedding habits, his rutting activity and virtually any routine in the life of a buck.

Contrary to what some hunters think, all deer are on some kind of travel pattern. Deer do not aimlessly roam the countryside

Understanding the travel patterns of monster bucks like this book-class deer is indeed a challenge. Checking out the available buck sign in the area is certainly essential, but we must also be able to predict movement patterns from advance knowledge and predictable tendencies to successfully unravel the secretive patterns of big nocturnal bucks. Photo by Bill Kinney.

without purpose to their travel. Instead, there are reasons as to when and why they do what they do. We can identify many of these influences and predict the effect they will have on the movement pattern. Consequently, with understanding, knowledge, an observant eye, experience and common sense, we can predict travel patterns with varying degrees of accuracy during different times of the season. Deer everywhere can be patterned, regardless of the conditions, time of year or terrain. We may not always have enough information to fully figure it out, but the pattern is there nonetheless.

Our skill in understanding and predicting travel patterns will certainly improve with practice and experience. A real key is having an observant eye so the clues can be quickly and accurately picked up. We must continually strive to better understand these patterns and improve our ability to put it all together since we're certain to

Guy Shanks took this near-book, 24-inch, Montana 11-pointer in the fall of 1991 after the discovery of huge rubs the previous spring. That fall, Guy figured out a great deal about his travel pattern and killed him in a rut area with a high density of big rubs and scrapes. Photo by author.

encounter many variations. Elements such as hunting pressure, rut periods, weather, terrain types, etc. create a myriad of influences that collectively affect travel patterns. On a case-by-case basis, we must be able to unravel each buck's particular pattern.

From a hunting standpoint, it is virtually impossible to be successful for big bucks year after year without knowing something about their travel patterns. Pure exposure in areas where lots of big bucks live might yield occasional opportunities, but to be consistent to any degree, a logical game plan based on an understanding and knowledge of travel patterns must be applied.

"Reverse sign reading"

One of the fundamental concepts in this book is what I call

All bucks are on some type of travel pattern, but unfortunately, a substantial portion of their movement may be done at night, making them difficult to both pattern and hunt. Fortunately for us, the breeding ritual, which this buck and doe are hotly engaged in, often brings out the "big boys" during daylight hours. Photo by Erwin & Peggy Bauer.

"reverse sign reading," which is simply predicting what deer should be doing at a given time under certain circumstances and then using sign to verify the assumption. This, of course, requires that one understand travel patterns and be able to predict them. In the "old school" of thinking, stand locations and tactics are selected based solely on the sign present, which usually includes tracks, trails, rubs, scrapes, droppings, etc. The presence of such sign reflects a pattern of what those deer or bucks had been doing in the past, but it does not necessarily predict the pattern they will be on the next day, week or month ... or more to the point, by the time you get your stand up.

In most cases, it takes one to two weeks of repeated use over the same travel route for a buck to leave enough sign for a hunter to distinguish a travel pattern. When we depend only on visible sign, we are counting on being able to predict future travel routes based on what the buck did in the past. In some cases, that works fine. Often, though, a change in the buck's travel pattern may well be underway, or could have already taken place, by the time the sign is clear enough for us to tell what he has been doing. In this case, sign may not reflect his current pattern and certainly not his future pattern. Reverse sign reading means anticipating changing travel patterns based on knowing what patterns should be underway at any given point in the four periods of the rut and under various other conditions, then using sign to verify the patterns we suspect.

Let's illustrate reverse sign reading by using a food source pattern as an example. Scouting might have revealed that bucks were using a soybean field in late summer, but based on knowledge of travel patterns, we would have predicted that the bucks will shift to acorns around the first of October. If the sign is the sole basis for predicting the current pattern, we may have opted to hunt near the field when hunting season opened, say, on October 1. In our example, however, the bucks would have already shifted to an acorn pattern. By using reverse sign reading, we would have applied this knowledge of changing food preferences and looked for fresh sign in the acorn groves to reinforce what we suspected.

The beauty of reverse sign reading — patterning — is that we don't have to reinvent the wheel at every turn. Much of what we need to know about travel patterns, such as movement tendencies in different periods of the rut, where bucks prefer to bed, which trails they use and preferred food sources at different times of the season, can be learned and predicted each year. Depending on how well you know the area, it may not even be necessary to rely on sign reading to reaffirm what we can already know.

Sign reading obviously plays a key role in accurately predicting both past and future travel patterns, but the real value and proper use of sign can be missed. Quite often, the mistake is made when "good" sign is discovered, and that sign then becomes the object or location hunted. The real value of sign lies in the fact that it defines, outlines and points out some regular and predictable line of travel, and we must keep in mind that it's the travel pattern, not the sign itself, that we should be hunting.

Obviously, there are many points along a buck's route of travel where he might be hunted successfully, but without question, some are far better than others. Sign might turn out to be present at the best stand site, but not necessarily. Any given sign is just part of a bigger picture, one piece of physical evidence that can be used to define an overall travel pattern of where and how a buck moves throughout his range. Sign helps us define a buck's pattern, then we must use common sense to figure out the best place and tactic to hunt that pattern.

Chapter 5

Family Units–
The Hub Of
Deer Society

AS WE BEGIN TO EXPLORE WHITETAIL TRAVEL PATTERNS, the need to understand the breeding ritual and social composition of the herd becomes clear. It is virtually impossible to predict travel patterns reliably if we don't understand certain basic concepts. For starters, we need to take a close look at the role of the family unit and the way in which it governs whitetail "society."

In the last decade, we've made giant strides in understanding the life cycle of this secretive species. Magazines such as *North American WHITETAIL* have probed into new realms of deer behavior; informative books have been written; universities and other groups have engaged in research studies; videos have captured whitetails in moments unseen by most hunters; and the hunting population has become much more knowledgeable overall. But even with all of the many sources of information, many hunters continue to harbor misconceptions about the social composition of a herd and its breeding ritual. The makeup and role of the family unit are among the least understood of all aspects of whitetail society.

At the heart of the whitetail's society is the family unit, which is made up of a "loose" group of related does and young bucks. Actually, the young bucks are forced out of the family unit sometime during their second year. Interestingly, the family units, not the mature bucks, occupy the best habitat in the area. Photo by Roman Jaskolski.

The family unit

A family unit might be described as a loose group of related females and young bucks that share a specific core area and habitat. Young bucks in this group are in a transitory state. They are forced out of the area at weaning age, but other newborn bucks immediately take their place. Technically, the "permanent" family unit is comprised exclusively of females since male offspring are residents for

Food, cover, plenty of edge — this is a classic set-up to harbor a family unit. Photo by author.

only a relatively short time.

It is important to understand that all events and structures in nature serve a purpose. They do not occur without some logical basis for their existence. The whitetail family unit is no exception. In fact, it's difficult even to define the family unit without also describing its social purpose.

If we think about the various places we hunt, we realize that does do not live in random locations. Rather, they live in "pockets" that generally include some of the most prime habitat in the area. The locations and boundaries of each group usually remain constant for years unless such elements as food sources or security cover change radically.

Where the family units live

Perhaps the single most important reason for the existence of the family unit is to ensure that reproducing females can occupy the most prime habitat in any given area. Once breeding has taken place, the does are solely responsible for rearing the offspring. Unlike birds and some other species in which the male shares in the process, the female deer handles this function alone. For this reason, she is "privileged" to occupy the most prime portions of the habitat. This is essential because fawn survival depends upon the mother's ability to consume large quantities of high-quality feed for milk production. Fawn survival is obviously more important to whitetail society than is the buck's need for high-quality feed for the growth of antlers.

Prime portions of the habitat (the most ideal core areas) are selected by the females and, as noted, are dominated for years. These generally are areas in which the most prime food sources connect to the most desirable cover, and the combination of the two defines the boundaries. Family units might exist within a few hundred yards of each other; in fact, their ranges may even overlap if deer densities are high. Or where densities are low, they might be found miles apart, especially in wilderness regions.

Where the terrain is broken with numerous small fields and plentiful cover, the average number of deer in a family unit might be low — perhaps 10 or even fewer. But in situations in which food sources are far apart and/or cover is limited, there might be as many as 50 or more females occupying the same core area. Typically, "broken" farm country with numerous fields and abundant, small woodlots will have family units that are smaller in number, and the groups will be more closely bunched. In farm country with vast fields and relatively small amounts of widely scattered cover, as well as in most wilderness areas, family units often are located from one to three miles apart.

The purpose of the family unit

Before proceeding, I need to define a couple of terms — "high-interaction areas" and "staging areas." Staging areas are specific places where deer bunch up prior to entering major food sources or other high-use areas. High-interaction areas are specific places where deer come together frequently and in numbers and where they engage in social and breeding rituals. Staging areas are a principle type of high-interaction area, but high-interaction areas can include places other than just staging areas. The importance of these terms will soon become apparent.

The family unit also plays a major social role and is of great significance to the breeding process. It's important to realize that for the relatively few dominant males in the population to breed 100 percent of the females — which is the objective in any big game population — those prime males must be able to locate and assess the condition of many does in a short period of time. They could not do this if the female population lived at randomly scattered locations.

The buck's monitoring of the breeding condition of the does is further facilitated by the existence of high-interaction areas located within the family unit's core area. Not only can bucks wander from one family unit to another to search for receptive does, they can go to specific high-interaction areas, which are frequently staging areas, at certain times of the day to find concentrations of does or to assess scent left by them.

In the natural scheme of things, this ensures that the "right" bucks will be able to find the "right" does when the time comes. The scrape itself is the most likely actual meeting place and is most often located in a high-interaction area, which in turn is located within the family unit's core area. In this arrangement bucks and does have a predetermined place to meet, which improves the odds of the prospective mates being able to find each other.

The family unit serves as a sort of permanent social structure and element of stability in the life of the whitetail. A buck spends most of his time in a much larger core area — often a square mile or more — and is the "traveler" or "searcher" during the breeding period. During this period, a buck's range of travel might jump from one or two miles within a 24-hour period to 10 or even 20. These traveling bucks are not wandering at random but are moving directly from one family unit to another to maximize their exposure to females. Obviously, if the does also were wandering in such a large pattern, the odds would work against the "right" bucks finding the "right" does.

The home range of the family unit is, as noted, relatively stable; thus, it serves year after year as the location where a specific group of females can be found. High-interaction areas tend to be located in the same areas each year. As bucks get older, they become more familiar with the location of additional family units. They also travel

During the summer and very early fall, bucks band together in what is known as "bachelor" groups, which normally consist of from two to six bucks of similar ages. In these groups, the bucks become familiar with each other and establish dominance ranking in a nonlethal way. Photo by Bill Kinney.

farther to monitor a greater number of females and, in effect, become more proficient breeders.

Many hunters are aware of the quest for dominance among bucks, but the same hierarchy exists among does as well. All deer, male or female, are rigidly structured in their dominance ranking, and the females are at least equal determinants of "who breeds whom." Actual selection of breeding partners is initiated by the more dominant female, as she selects the scrape (scent-marked by a specific male) and, consequently, the buck of her choice.

Where the prime feed is, the family units will be also, assuming the necessary cover is present. Note the young buck in this bunch of does — the family unit's matriarch doe is sure to make him feel unwelcome soon. Photo by Bill Marchel.

Here, the family unit plays an important role by allowing a group of females numerous opportunities for interaction. This establishes the overall dominance ranking. Bucks accomplish the same function when they form their bachelor groups in the summer months. These few months of interaction among similar-aged males allow them to find their individual dominance rank without resorting to fierce (and potentially lethal) antler-to-antler combat. As a result, as breeding season approaches, both males and females, in their respective manners, have a social rank that accounts for all individuals.

Within its boundaries, the core area of each family unit can have a varying number of high-interaction areas or staging areas. These also can differ in the amount of activity each is receiving, but usually, there will be one to three primary locations where as much as 90 percent of the activity occurs. The family unit and high-interaction areas are present for a specific reason, but both actually are formed according to the geography of the land and the relationship of prime food sources and ideal security cover/bedding areas.

Consequently, high-interaction areas are located according to the travel patterns between those food sources and bedding areas.

For example, as the does leave the bedding area and travel toward the primary food source, they generally move right along until they reach a "staging" area, a place where they can browse and spend some time before entering the relatively open feeding area. Typically, the staging areas, a type of high-interaction zone, are anywhere from 20 to 200 yards inside the cover and often are near water or other sites with prime browse and adequate cover. Late in the afternoon, deer move to these areas, browse until nearly sunset, then move into the main feeding area as they feel comfortable. In the morning, they reverse the pattern by leaving the field near daylight, moving into the staging area to browse awhile then traveling directly to the bedding area.

Over a period of time, bucks also become familiar with these staging areas, or other types of high-interaction zones. They know in advance of the breeding period that these places of concentrated activity and high use by the does are the best places to find receptive does. As the actual breeding period draws nearer the bucks spend more time here and spend less in areas of marginal doe activity. The buck's use of these areas increases as the pre-breeding period progresses, and eventually, these staging areas become the social hotspot for the herd. However, this only occurs at a certain point of the season, which we'll discuss later.

How family units are formed

Now that we know the role of the family unit, we need to understand how it is formed. Obviously, all deer would like to occupy the most prime habitat, so how are the does able to pull it off? How can the bucks be made to occupy a less desirable portion of the habitat when they are usually dominant over does? Simple!

Just as most humans grow up in a certain locale where they put down roots, a deer likewise establishes its "home" early in life. This place is what we call a "core area." A strange occurrence at weaning age is at the root of core-area establishment. Let's say a doe has a pair of fawns, one male and one female. Sometime before the doe's next fawns are born and before the weaning of the current pair takes place, the female fawn will adopt and "imprint" the core area of her mother. The same feeding and bedding areas will be used, as will trails, high-interaction areas, travel corridors, winter and summer ranges, etc. She is another potential fawn-bearing member of the population and will be allowed to live among the other females and share the same prime habitat, though exactly which part of that "territory" she inherits will depend on her own dominance ranking within the family unit.

The male fawn, on the other hand, is eventually forced out of his childhood home by his own mother and other females of the group. He will vacate the area and set up residence — imprint — in a new core area well away from that of his mother. Just how far do these year-old bucks go? A whitetail biologist in Iowa once told me of an experiment in which his department had radio-collared young bucks before weaning so their movement could be studied. The biologists found that a few bucks traveled as far as 70 miles to establish their core areas, and the majority moved 5 to 20 miles! Now, I don't profess to know how far the "average" exiled buck is relocating, but I suspect most are moving at least a mile to five miles. Regardless of the exact distance, it's safe to assume that the buck does not adopt the same core area as his mother and that their core areas will not overlap, barring exceptional circumstances.

Such a social and reproductive scheme also has another reason for its existence — dispersal of the gene pool. Obviously, if buck fawns were allowed to adopt the core areas of their mothers, inbreeding would occur; nothing would prevent a buck from eventually breeding his mother, sister, etc. So, nature sends the buck to another area where there are unrelated females.

As these bucks mature and become breeders in their respective areas, genes are spread around and inbreeding becomes unlikely. Research has shown that the whitetail population across North America displays enormous genetic variability, which is one reason the species has proved so adaptable in the face of changing habitat conditions. A social structure that leads to dispersal of the breeding males is the best way for a species to accomplish this.

Of course, there's still plenty we don't know about the dynamics of whitetail family units. However, from a hunter's perspective, the main point is that these female-oriented groups exist and that they have a profound effect on where and how we should hunt.

Understanding the concept of family units gives us a distinct edge in predicting a buck's travel pattern and helps us to better understand the complex breeding ritual.

Chapter 6

Buck Core Areas–
The Inner Sanctuary

IT SHOULD BE OBVIOUS THAT without knowing where a buck wants to go and why he wants to go there, we have no real basis for predicting travel patterns. Of course, many factors affect how travel patterns evolve and the way in which they are used. But no matter what the details of a buck's travel pattern, that pattern revolves around his core area, the most "comfortable" part of the animal's home range.

As we saw in the previous chapter, a mature buck's core area can (and usually will) be some distance from the place where he was born. Nonetheless, it serves as his adopted or imprinted home and is the place where most of his adult life is spent.

A buck's core area makes up only a fraction of his entire home range. We've all heard that old saying, "A whitetail buck lives his whole life in one square mile," but we now know this seldom is true. There are many instances when and reasons why bucks leave their core area and travel widely.

Still, in many cases, a buck will spend the bulk of his adult life — as much as 90 percent of it — within an area not much larger than a square mile. This broad statement is true in most parts of the species' range, but the "square mile" tends to get larger in certain terrain types or where severe climate forces deer to migrate between summer and winter ranges. Buck core areas in the North tend to be larger, in general, than do those in the South. Also, as the terrain

A buck's pattern revolves around his core area, which is the most secure and "comfortable" part of his home range. This is where he spends as much as 90 percent of his time, and he nearly always beds there, unless forced out or lured away by the rut. Photo by author.

becomes more open, core areas generally become larger. Finally, a buck core area also will tend to be smaller where prime food sources are found close together.

Why bucks travel outside their home area

Bucks spend most of their time in restricted core areas because it is their "home" imprinted from an early age and their everyday needs are met there. However, at various times throughout the year, a buck will travel outside this home for one or more of the following reasons:

(1) The rut. When the time for breeding approaches, a buck will look wherever he can for potential mates, and this search frequently takes him outside of his core area. How frequently he engages in such travel will be influenced greatly by the number and age of other local bucks (which affect the amount of competition for breeding rights); the deer density (which affects the spacing of fami-

This is a wide buck — 28 1/4 inches! The author shot this big Alberta buck early in the season after finding his sign and deducing that he was bedding on a nearby knob. The buck met his end as he doubled back during a small drive. Photo by author.

ly units); and assorted other factors.

(2) Nutritional requirements. During the period of rapid antler growth and the buildup of body fat for the winter, bucks require an especially protein-rich, high-quality diet. Often, when such food sources are not available within the core area, a buck will travel a substantial distance to find one. Travel of this nature generally occurs from sometime in June on into August or possibly even early September.

Overall nutritional stress can occur in either the winter or the summer, depending on the location. (In some areas, it might even occur during both of those seasons.) In northern regions in particular, there can be a dramatic shift in the location of prime food sources from summer/fall to winter/spring. Travel outside the core area might be required in order for the buck to survive the winter. On the other end of the spectrum, in some places (such as parts of Texas and the South), the predominant stress period for whitetails is often in the summer, when drought can hamper the growth of forage. Again, the buck goes wherever he needs to within his overall range to find enough food to get over the hump.

(3) Security. Obviously, there are many types of deer habitat across North America. Some offer large blocks of adequate cover, while others don't. And, the degree of hunting pressure varies radically from one area to another, and it generally is not tied to the amount of cover present. In many areas, hunting pressure intensifies at some point of the season to levels so extreme that bucks might leave their core areas in search of greater security.

(4) Other influences of man and nature. Many other events intrude upon the lives of bucks and can force them to leave their core areas. Logging operations, forest fires, annual flooding, crop rotation, clearing of land for development, farming and the loss of habitat in general occasionally force bucks — temporarily or permanently — from their core areas.

As a general rule, bucks, especially mature bucks, do not want to socialize with does during most of the year. Exceptions occur when prime food sources are scarce and/or isolated, where deer densities are too high and when the rut kicks in. Such situations force bucks and does to share parts of a common core area. If given a choice, however, a buck will establish and maintain his own core area outside the core area of any family unit. The core areas of different bucks are more likely to overlap than are those of a buck and a family unit. Generally, buck core areas are perhaps twice the size of those occupied by doe groups.

Establishing a core area

When a year-old buck "hits the road" in search of a core area to call home, what governs his decision on where to go? Why might he end up seven miles north of where he was born rather than seven miles south? I suspect that as bucks make their first exploratory forays into the "outside world" at around the age of 1 to 1 1/2 years, they do look in various directions. However, we might never fully understand which factors are most important in their final decision of where to stake out a "territory." Of course, each year new vacancies are created as other deer, including mature bucks, are harvested by hunters or die from natural causes. No doubt this opens up some available habitat for the establishment of core areas by yearling bucks.

Varying habitat types create different situations that greatly affect where bucks can go to seek unfilled niches. For example, let's look at mountainous western Montana. The many relatively fertile valleys are the most desirable habitat and traditionally have been the "primary" whitetail range in this region. But, the herd has grown considerably in recent years, so in order to find unoccupied habitat, young bucks now are being forced to leave the valleys and move higher and higher onto the surrounding mountainsides, where food is far less abundant.

A similar scenario occurs in western and central Canada. There, the whitetail population has increased on the "fringe" between farmland and the huge provincial forests, which stretches unbroken for hundreds of miles. Now, family units are occupying most of the prime habitat along the fringe, forcing bucks deeper and deeper into the "wilderness" to establish core areas. We even can see this type of situation in areas of Louisiana where farmland butts up against huge swamps of mature trees that offer relatively little deer browse.

Things are somewhat different in many portions of the U.S., however, because the habitat is more homogenous and whitetails are more evenly distributed. In such places, there now are few or no areas without some kind of deer population. Also, in certain parts of the Midwest or Southeast, broken farmland sometimes stretches for mile after mile, providing whitetails with abundant feeding options and cover. Because some of these herds have now existed for many years, virtually all of the obvious core-area niches have been taken and few choice spots are available.

The unsettled nature of a buck's life as he enters his first really vulnerable hunting season (age 1 1/2 years) is a big part of what makes him an easy target. Not only are these yearling bucks far more plentiful than older bucks, they are relatively naive. Add in the fact that these young bucks also are in the process of finding and learning new living quarters, sometimes called the "fall shuffle," and it's easy to see why they are highly susceptible to hunting pressure. No wonder the buck harvest in nearly every part of North America is made up predominantly of yearlings.

In their second year, bucks are forced from the family unit and move out to establish their own core area, which may be miles away from where they were born and raised. This is one of the ways that nature assures genetic dispersion. Photo by Roman Jaskolski.

The buck's "luck" factor

Many times I've heard hunters say, "That old buck is really smart. He lives up on the mountain (or deep in the swamp) where nobody can bother him." Not surprisingly, many such bucks never do get killed and simply die of old age. Yet, when it comes to their choice of a core area, are they really smart or mostly just lucky? I believe it's usually the latter. In my opinion, these "smart" bucks are actually no more intelligent than any others.

Most bucks that have chosen particularly safe core areas as yearlings have not done so because they somehow envisioned that they would one day be subjected to hunting pressure. Instead, because of the many factors described thus far, some will end up in places that later will get a lot of hunting pressure, while others won't. For a buck to establish a core area in a heavily pressured area and then manage to avoid hunters long enough to reach the prime trophy ages of 4 1/2 years or more, he must overcome astronomical odds. A few do, but not many.

In contrast, let's look at the "lucky" yearling buck that chooses a less desirable core area "on top of the mountain" or "deep in the swamp." As a result of his almost arbitrary choice, he faces relatively little hunting pressure each fall and that dramatically raises his chances of survival. As long as the buck hangs in or very near his isolated core area, he stands a fair chance of avoiding hunters.

As we compare these two types of core areas, we see that over a period of years there is a distinct difference in the turnover of bucks. In heavily hunted, vulnerable locations, bucks are harvested at a young age, thus creating more vacancies for the next year's crop of relocating yearlings. The cycle simply repeats itself until the pressure patterns change and the age structure and other dynamics of the herd are altered. Meanwhile, the "lucky" bucks that set up shop in lightly hunted locations have a higher survival rate. This can create pockets with higher average age bucks. Obviously, these are hotspots for mature bucks, but these are not the easiest deer to locate or pattern.

For all practical purposes, bucks that have core areas on unhuntable land, such as a state park, enjoy many of the same advantages as their wilderness counterparts. From the hunter's perspective, it matters not whether the core area is way up on the side of a steep, timbered mountain or on the wrong side of a property line. The result is the same — reduced odds of catching the buck in a vulnerable position. In such situations, we should try to look for factors that will make the buck easier to hunt by luring him out of his usual stomping grounds.

Core areas and hunting strategy

Much of the year in those "less desirable" habitats, such as a mountainside or thicket far from the fertile waterway, the buck is somewhat isolated from prime food sources, as well as from does. As noted, food and does are two of the primary reasons he occasionally leaves the core area and enters areas to which we have better access as hunters. Unfortunately, from a hunting perspective, there seldom is much nutritional stress on bucks when hunting seasons are open. Some very early seasons do get underway prior to the time of velvet shedding in late summer, but they generally start at about the time bucks are returning to their core areas anyway. A few seasons are late

The rut, nutritional requirements and security are some of the reasons a buck will travel outside his core area. When a wise, old buck is firmly entrenched in his core area and mostly nocturnal, forced movement is about the only way to get him to expose himself. Photo by Bill Marchel.

enough into winter that the hunter might encounter stressed bucks that are taking advantage of special feeding situations, but these are uncommon. In neither type of scenario are bucks living in protected/isolated core areas especially vulnerable to hunters for lengthy periods because of the need to feed.

However, things are quite different during the rut, when many hunting seasons are in progress. Most bucks, especially the more mature ones, are going to leave their core areas off and on for at least three to four weeks each fall in search of "hot" does. How far and how often these bucks range out of their core areas depends largely on the doe density and the amount of buck competition within the area. More competition for breeding rights will cause bucks to travel farther and more frequently.

Hunting bucks with core areas located well away from places with high deer densities can be quite productive because many of these bucks are sure to be older and larger. But, the bad news is that these deer also can be frustrating to hunt. In order to score on one of these bucks, you first must be able to recognize the situation. Secondly, you must be able to read and decipher sign well enough to get a handle on the buck's travel pattern.

From talking with literally thousands of whitetail hunters across North America, I have concluded that one of the most common problems in hunting trophy bucks is that hunters see only sign of the deer but not the animals that make it. For example, it is common for a hunter to locate one or more big rubs on his hunting property but never even get a glimpse of the buck that did the damage. This can be because the buck is largely nocturnal; however, that isn't necessarily the case. Often, the hunter is being overly conservative in his view of the buck's travels. In other words, he's trying to pattern the buck in too small an area. Some hunters are studying the sign on a couple of hundred acres and trying to put together a picture of the buck's activity, when the buck himself is working an area of several square miles.

A second common problem occurs when the hunter is finding buck sign in one or more locations far from the animal's core area. The deer is simply not there for many days out of the year. One of the best examples is the common mistake of spotting a buck in an open field in the summer when the need for high-quality forage might have lured him there from a core area several miles away. Once the buck sheds his velvet in late summer, he might make a few rubs in or around the feeding location before moving back to his actual core area. A hunter should look for indications that the buck has not only made early rubs but has continued to rub in the area. If that proves not to be the case, there is reason to believe the deer has moved back "home."

Big rubs that show up in an area only just prior to or during the rut also can indicate that the buck is coming in from a distant core area. During the last several years, I've found many "hotspots" after the season, areas loaded with huge rubs and numerous scrapes. But in my early scouting the following September or October, these bucks were nowhere to be found in those same areas. They simply didn't live there! But then, usually around November 5 to 10, huge fresh rubs would again appear, often on the same trees, indicating that the bucks were traveling substantial distances to work these doe areas at night. During the last two or three weeks of November (the breeding period in that area), these bucks actually could be hunted successfully in those doe areas; however, by early December, they would have abandoned their rutting areas and moved back to their core areas to rest up.

All of this points out why a good working knowledge of core areas is extremely important for every trophy hunter. The core area is essentially the one fixed point to which the buck always will return at various times throughout the year. It's the only part of his travel pattern we can predict with almost unfailing certainty on a year-to-year basis.

Chapter 7

The All-Important Breeding Ritual

ACCURATELY PREDICTING THE TRAVEL PATTERNS of mature whitetail bucks requires that we thoroughly understand many aspects of the species' behavior, particularly those regarding the rut. In virtually every part of North America, the rut falls in some portion of hunting season, and it should be obvious to anyone that deer behavior is radically affected by the breeding urge. Not only do we need a good working knowledge of the biology behind the reproductive cycle, we also must be able to recognize the sometimes subtle clues that help us analyze the status of the rut and its effect on the local herd. Without being able to do this, we can't get any advantage on the buck, and we're reduced to merely hoping that he'll eventually blunder into our sights.

A different kind of breeding scheme

The whitetail is without question one of the most adaptable animals on earth. In terms of being able to make a living under varying conditions, this species stands out as not only being able to survive but actually thrive — sometimes against unbelievable odds.

Yes, the whitetail has been able to evolve/adapt to a multitude of habitats, climatic conditions, diseases, harvest techniques and other changes, many of them the sort of "problems" that have caused a variety of other big game species to decline since the days of Columbus. The difference that sets the whitetail apart from all other big game is its breeding system, which is in many ways unique.

Although the increased activity by bucks during the rut makes them more vulnerable, accurately predicting their travel patterns during the breeding period is more difficult than during any other period. Photo by Bill Marchel.

I'm not exactly certain of all the ways this contributes to the species' adaptability, but it is no coincidence that the single most successful big game animal has a one-of-a-kind reproductive process.

Undoubtedly, this unique breeding scheme allows the whitetail to directly out-compete the mule deer in areas where both species are found, including portions of the Great Plains, Rocky Mountains, western Canada and the Southwest. Whitetails in these regions today are prospering at the expense of mulies, in some cases actually replacing them on a widespread basis. I believe this occurs not only because of greater adaptability on the part of the whitetail but also because of its breeding system. Whitetails actually have bred the mulies out of house and home — quite literally.

Mule deer are polygamous breeders, meaning the most dominant males gather harems of females and breed them as they become receptive. This is the case with most other hoofed big game animals in the world, including elk, sheep, antelope, moose, etc. Of course, in these species as well as the whitetail, the objective is the same — for the most dominant males to breed the females. Depending upon many factors, approximately 20 percent of the males, the most dominant ones, should breed 100 percent of the sexually mature females. In well-balanced healthy populations of any of these species, that is exactly what happens. This is nature's way of assuring that the most superior, healthy genes for species survival are passed on to the next generation.

Nature's scheme is also clever in allowing only about 10 percent of the females to become receptive at any given time. This increases the chances that the dominant males will have the opportunity to breed them. Depending upon the species, females may be receptive for 24 to 48 hours on average, which means the same male theoretically could breed one every day or two. If a breeding period is 15 days, which is average for many big game species, including whitetails, this means a male theoretically could breed 7 to 15 females during the entire period.

For species such as elk, this is possible because a dominant herd bull may control 15 cows, and he can breed most of them. Twenty percent of all bull elk can effectively control most of the cows, and the top males do most of the breeding.

In whitetails, the same objective is accomplished but in a much different fashion. The whitetail buck is what I call a "monogamous" breeder, though he is not in the strictest sense of the word. He does not mate for life with a single female, but breeds and focuses his breeding activity on only one female at a time. As with the polygamous breeders, the plan is for only the most dominant males to breed 100 percent of the females.

Now, before going forward, this a good place to explain how the term "buck:doe ratio" is used in this book. From purely a scientific standpoint, the buck:ratio is the number of adult (1 1/2-year-old animals and older) bucks versus the number of adult does entering the fall (September) population. However, the most critical aspect of buck:doe ratios comes during the actual breeding period, which occurs later in the fall when both natural and man-caused mortality (hunting season has often been in for a while before breeding

Ken Contley killed this huge 13-point Saskatchewan non-typical as he was checking does at a food source. This battle-scarred warhorse broke two points from fighting between the time Ken first spotted the buck and the day he killed him a week later, indicating high buck competition. Photo by author.

begins) have taken an addition toll on the buck population. As a result, the buck:doe ratio at the critical breeding period can be substantially poorer than that of September. Since I consider the buck:doe ratio during the breeding period to be of more significance than in September, I prefer to give buck:doe ratios at the time of breeding, which is exactly what I do throughout this book.

With that, let's resume our look at the whitetail breeding scheme. For illustrative purposes, assume we have a herd with a buck:doe ratio that's essentially equal (1:1). When breeding begins, again as with other big game, no more than 10 percent of the females normally come into estrus at a given time. If a particular herd contains 100 bucks and 100 does, and 10 percent of the females are receptive at any given time during the breeding period, 10 does

The exchange of scent information at visual "signposts" is done primarily through rubs and scrapes. Here, a buck scent marks an overhanging branch at a scrape. Photo by Neal & Mary Jane Mishler.

will be in heat at any particular time throughout the breeding period. It's almost certain that the 10 most dominant or highest ranked bucks will end up doing most of the breeding in this herd.

Here we see a weakness in the armor of the monogamous reproductive process of the whitetail. Buck:doe ratios affect the long-term gene pool and inevitable buck quality much more than with polygamous big-game species.

Independent of other factors, the natural mortality rate of bucks is always higher than for does. Some of the causes are fighting and increased exposure to vehicles and predators during the extensive travel of the rut itself. Thus, a 1:1 ratio is unrealistic, even in a natural, unhunted herd. One buck per two does is a more common occurrence. So, let's look at a herd with 100 bucks and 200 does. At any given time during the breeding period, we would assume that 20 does would be in estrus, meaning that 20 of the most dominant bucks would do most of the breeding. This is probably a more realistic scenario even in a lightly hunted herd unless intensive manage is applied.

Unfortunately, man is impacting the whitetail breeding scheme in a negative way by harvesting too many bucks and not enough does. Let's look at a real-world scenario to see the impact this can have on the reproductive process. Suppose we have a herd of 500 deer with a 1:4 ratio, giving us 100 bucks and 400 does. Ten percent of the 400 does is 40, so at any given time during the breeding period, 40 of the more dominant bucks (40 percent) now would have the chance to breed. Opportunity for breeding by more subordinate and possibly inferior males is obviously greater than in the more balanced herds previously discussed.

If the buck:doe ratio becomes unbalanced enough, there will be virtually no competition for breeding rights, as the number of receptive does at any given time during the breeding period might equal or exceed the number of mature bucks available to breed them. Suppose our deer herd has a total of 110 animals with a ratio of 1:10 — 10 bucks and 100 does. Ten percent of 100 is 10 receptive does, meaning all 10 bucks have an equal chance of breeding.

In this scenario, all buck genes, good or bad, are being passed on to the next generation. In some herds with extremely heavy pressure on the buck segment, there are now problems with a sizable number of does not being bred by any buck in their first estrus cycle. This becomes most likely when buck:doe ratios exceed 1:10. As a result, unbred does will cycle again in 28 days, at which time they will be bred in what is generally known as the "secondary" rut or second estrus cycle.

It's easy to see the effect this can have on a herd, especially when played out over a long period. Not only does the lack of buck competition result in unfit genetics having an opportunity to be passed on, a prolonged breeding period, caused by too few bucks being available to breed the does the first time, causes an extended fawning period. In many habitats, such as the far North and arid regions of South Texas, the window of maximum survival for fawns is rather short. If a fawn is born late in Manitoba, for example, it probably won't be big enough by the next winter to withstand the rigorous conditions. And, a late-born fawn in a drought-prone region puts a heavy milk demand on its mother during the late summer, when forage is scarce and generally of poor nutritional quality. This can have a dramatic impact on fawn survival.

The breeding ritual

The average hunter probably figures that the biggest bucks get their choice of does for breeding. While that's true in the sense that the dominant bucks normally get to do more of the breeding than subordinate bucks, it's critical for us to realize that the female, at least the dominant ones, actually chooses the male for breeding. All of the fanfare of rubs, scrapes and various physical displays are intended to impress her. In essence, then, it's the doe, not the buck, that actually controls the breeding.

The function of the "bachelor" grouping of bucks within similar age classes each summer is to provide interaction among males, whereby dominance ranking is primarily established by the "show" of antlers. Until the velvet is shed in late summer, little thought or attention is given to does. Bucks and does will interact some on feeding grounds they share, but as a rule, neither sex wants much to do with the other outside the rut.

The first sign of display to the opposite sex begins with rubs. Especially during the breeding season, deer have a need to communicate both physically and by scent. Other animals, such as foxes, coyotes, dogs and cats, choose prominent visual "signposts" already established in strategic places to communicate by scent. These can take the form of a corner fence post, fire hydrants, rocks, mounds of dirt or any other likely signpost. The key is that they are already established, and both males and females can "trade" scent information as to who's living and traveling through the area. Each animal is recognizable by his or her individual scent.

In the case of the whitetail, there are no pre-established signposts at which to trade such information. The buck must physically establish sites that will serve as accepted meeting places. This begins in the form of a rub on a prominently located tree. Undoubtedly, the buck is also working on trees and bushes to prepare neck and other muscles for fighting, as well as to gain a "blind feel" for where their rack is and how to use it. We must remember that a buck cannot see

The spot where scrapes are made is the primary place where bucks meet does when the time is right. Here, a giant non-typical works a scrape by pawing down to fresh dirt with his front feet. Photo by Bill Kinney.

much of his newly grown rack, so he can only learn its configuration and develop reflexes by touching it against something, primarily trees and bushes.

Rubs serve as both visual signposts and scent signposts where scent communication can occur. Initially, bucks tend to establish their own individual lines of rubs, marking each tree with the frontal gland located on the forehead. Early rubs tend to define a buck's travel routes and his overall travel range. As the season progresses, however, rubs tend to be concentrated in portions of the range of family units, and specifically in the high-interaction areas. Eventually, all bucks will tend to work many of the same, prominent trees located in key areas. At this point, bucks are using a somewhat subtle form of advertising their presence since they know breeding is still quite a while in coming.

As testosterone levels rise in the bucks, they become more enthused by the prospects of breeding and escalate their advertising to the next level — the establishment of scrapes. At first, scrapes are made in a more random fashion. As time passes, however, scraping

This big buck is urinating over his "hocks," or tarsal glands, in a scrape. His particular "signature" scent from the hock glands is picked up by the urine then passed on to the scrape, leaving his individual mark to advertise his presence to any does in the area. Photo by Neal & Mary Jane Mishler.

activity begins to shift progressively toward the family units, and ultimately to the high-interaction areas. Just prior to the first does becoming receptive, almost all scrape activity and monitoring will occur within these high-interaction areas.

The scrape serves the purpose of providing more specific scent information and pre-establishes a meeting place where the "proper" doe can find the "proper" buck. "Proper" in this case means that the more dominant does seek out the more dominant males by using scent to determine which scrapes are used by particular bucks. As most hunters know, the scrape is a pawed-out oval area on the ground, almost always under an overhanging branch approximately the height above the ground of the buck's face or antlers. Most scrapes are intentionally established in strategic locations where bucks feel sure does will pass by them.

Generally, bucks will work overhanging branches with their antlers and frontal glands to leave their individual scent. They also will rub the sides of their faces on their hock (tarsal) glands, then rub their faces on the branches, which further scent-marks the scrape. Some of the branches are bitten off to provide a blunt end on the branches, which makes it easier for the buck to mark them. The buck often uses his tongue in the process, possibly to leave further scent information through saliva, thought its true significance is uncertain. The final scent is left after a fresh pawing of the ground takes place and the buck urinates over his tarsal glands, rear legs held together, into the scrape. He then heads off to the next one.

As stated, initial scrapes tend to be located at random, but they become focused and intensified in high-interaction areas as the time for breeding draws near. In the latter part of the pre-breeding period, bucks will abandon many of their earlier "scattered" scrapes and travel greater distances to work those located in high-interaction areas. In doing so, they will visit a much greater number of family units. Eventually, a buck will establish a pattern of scrape visitation, which is known as a scrape line.

Studies utilizing infrared photography to monitor scrapes over 24-hour periods have shown that does actually spend more time at and around scrapes than do bucks. Obviously, the females are interested in which males are visiting those meeting places, so scent communication is occurring over a fairly long period. Through this scrape phenomenon, bucks still are putting their best foot forward, vying for the affection of the females.

Does also urinate in and around the scrape area, affording the bucks the opportunity to monitor their breeding condition. Through the urine, bucks can determine the amount of estrogen content, which in turn affects his activity. As the estrogen level increases, bucks focus their scrape activity in the high-interaction areas near the highest concentrations of does. As the time for breeding nears, a dominant buck usually will relocate his bedding area relatively near to his primary scrape line within the high-interaction area. Now, he frequently checks scrapes, concentrating his watch around those he considers to be the hottest prospects during the final days before does actually come into heat. I doubt that serious fighting often occurs over this "property", but big bucks certainly will chase off lesser bucks, especially during the last week prior to breeding. (An opportunity for rattling.)

As breeding nears, does are familiar with the locations of the scrapes of the bucks they've sensed as being most desirable for breeding partners. Several hours before a doe comes into heat, she urinates in the scrape of the buck of her choice. As he checks his scrape line, the buck now smells where the doe urinated and trails her. Often, she'll be waiting within a couple of hundred yards. Generally, the buck remains with her for 24 to 48 hours and exclusively breeds her, as long as he is dominant enough to fend off other bucks. Once she goes out of heat, he travels to other high-interaction areas in search of the next hot doe and checks scrapes there or, as often is the case, picks up another ready doe even while making his routes. This pattern continues until all sexually active females in the area have been bred or go out of heat.

We'll look into each of these phases of the rut in far more detail later and discuss the specifics of buck activity and how to find and interpret the relevant sign. But for now, the main point to remember is that there's a real difference between rutting activity and breeding itself. We will consider an overall time frame — during all of which activity is affected in one way or the other by the rut — that encompasses the entire time from velvet-shedding in the late summer through antler-casting in mid to late winter. In many parts of North America, all or most of this occurs during open season. Virtually throughout this time frame, bucks are reacting in some way or other to the opposite sex, but only for a short time is any breeding actually taking place. Fortunately, a buck need not be actively breeding for us to take advantage of his sexual urge. In fact, when hunting a specific buck, I'd far rather pursue him when he's not breeding. We'll see why later, but for now we need to realize that a big buck's instincts for rubbing, scraping, scent-checking does, fighting and trying to intimidate rival bucks are all behaviors that we hunters can take advantage of, even when no breeding is actually underway.

Obviously, if we don't understand what the breeding process involves and how its stages progress, we aren't going to know where or how to decipher travel patterns; nor will we know which types of observed behavior (either by bucks or does) are providing us with important clues. That definitely would diminish our chances of taking a mature buck because he doesn't just wander around the landscape at random. He's grown old by being reclusive and not follow-

This fresh, well-used scrape is probably large because it has been worked by numerous bucks, not because a large buck worked it. Such scrapes are hunting hotspots during the pre-breeding period. Photo by Bill Marchel.

ing the standard patterns of other deer. Yet, his preoccupation with the opposite sex for a few weeks each year gives us a real chance to catch him with his guard down. The hunter who consistently harvests big bucks recognizes this window of vulnerability and knows how to use it to his advantage.

Chapter 8

Sign And Sign Reading

T HE HEART OF MY PHILOSOPHY on hunting big bucks centers around the need to focus on an individual buck that meets our particular standard. Just the intelligent expenditure of time in a buck's range increases the odds simply through the "exposure factor." As more is learned about the buck's travel pattern, the odds become even higher as we identify his vulnerable points. Hopefully, we eventually will come to understand a great deal about his travel pattern. Then and only then will we have maximized our chances for success. Certainly, our ability to unravel and accurately predict travel patterns revolves around reading and understanding deer sign.

Two critical elements of a travel pattern are where and when the buck moves. Sign reading is especially vital in figuring out the "where" part. Our objective is to locate, identify and interpret sign to assist in the process of deciphering where (and why) a buck is traveling throughout his range. We then want to hunt him in the very best place over his entire pattern, not necessarily only where the most visible sign is. As we've said, the real value of sign is not for hunting purposes but to decipher travel patterns. When we happen upon promising buck sign and hunt it independent of full knowledge of his pattern, we are in essence hunting only a small segment of his overall pattern. This may be a good choice, but in all likelihood, it's not the best one.

As deer move about their range, they leave evidence of their presence. If a buck wants to get from Point A to Point B, he will choose a logical route based on cover, terrain, obstructions, etc. If

As bucks go about their daily lives and travel around their home range, they leave sign that helps us unravel their travel patterns. Photo by Bill Marchel.

other deer want to travel between the same two points, they are likely to use the same route. With repeated use, that route becomes a trail. The more frequently it is used, the more visible it becomes. Over a period of time, a network of trails is established.

Trails have specific origins and destinations. They do not weave aimlessly over the countryside. A trail may leave a favorite bedding area and end up at a popular food source. A "perimeter" trail may circle a field just inside the woods. Such a trail is usually created by bucks to intersect the paths of does as they make their way to a field. This is often evidenced by the fact that scrapes and rubs are found at intersections with other trails. In fact, each type of destination has its own mix of sign that will help identify what the deer were doing there. For instance, droppings, tracks, beds and rubs are likely evidence that the place is a bedding site. Cracked acorns, nipped-off vegetation and other feeding sign obviously point to a feeding area. In and around major feeding areas, you also will generally find numerous rubs, heavy trails, scrapes, droppings and evidence of heavy deer usage. Rut areas have relatively high numbers of rubs and

Sign reading is an acquired skill; not a natural talent. Time spent in the woods with an observant eye and a searching mind is the best educator. You're onto something when you find a rub like this one! Photo by Bill Marchel.

scrapes as well as running tracks indicating buck/doe rut interaction.

Rubs, scrapes and, to a degree, large tracks have special significance because they are created by bucks. This sign allows us to single out buck activity from general deer movement and provides us with vital information needed to locate and pattern an individual buck.

Locating and interpreting sign is not as straightforward as walking through the woods and seeing what turns up. Logic must be applied. There is too much country within a buck's range to visually inspect all of it, so we must anticipate the various destinations and even the location of the trails used to get back and forth. The first step is to become familiar with the topography and features of the land that will impact travel. Roads, fields, cover, travel corridors and such all influence travel patterns. Secondly, specific destination points, such as food sources, family units (doe concentrations), rut areas, etc., should be located. Once destination points are found, and substantiated by sign, the connecting trails should be sought out. This process is continued over a wide area until we have a feel for what the buck is doing.

Sign reading is an acquired skill; not a natural talent. Most inexperienced sign readers miss the majority of available sign because they simply don't recognize it or they look in the wrong places. Guidance from veterans is certainly helpful, but time spent in the woods with an observant eye and a searching mind is the ultimate educator.

Chapter 9

Factors Affecting Travel Patterns

MANY FACTORS INflUENCE HOW, WHEN AND WHERE deer movement takes place. Although each factor has its own unique influence, deer movement, including the specific travel patterns in place at a given time, is usually the result of several factors working together. Throughout the season, the factors influencing movement are constantly changing, thus altering movement patterns in one way or another. To better understand and predict these changing patterns, we must first understand how the individual factors affect movement.

Period of the rut

In each of the rut periods, the rise and ebb of the buck's urge to breed dramatically impacts activity and travel patterns. During the height of the sex drive, the pre-breeding and breeding period, the urge to mate is so strong that it frequently overrides other factors, even major ones like hunting pressure. Let's briefly examine how the breeding urge affects movement during each period.

During the "rut-preparation period," which begins at velvet-shedding (approximately September 1) and extends through mid-October (depending on the region), the bucks are on a predictable travel pattern, moving mostly from bedding to feeding areas. They are more interested in food than in does and normally reside within their core area. Bucks tend to travel relatively short distances, bed close to their food source and are likely to be somewhat nocturnal.

The "pre-breeding period" begins as a gradual transition

This 26-inch, Manitoba 13-pointer made the mistake of trailing a doe into the open just as the rut was starting up. The author had seen the buck earlier and had hunted him for three straight days before the buck slipped up. Photo by author.

around the middle of October and continues through approximately November 10 on average. Bucks now are more interested in does than food. They spend much more time traveling, going from one high-interaction area to another as they work scrapes and check does for the first sign of estrus. Generally, they still bed in their core area and continue to be fairly predictable in their movement.

The "breeding period" is a relatively short two-week period that begins around November 10 and ends about Thanksgiving over much of the country. Bucks are now totally focused on does. Travel patterns are unpredictable, and bucks now cover a lot of country, often in daylight hours. The bigger bucks are likely to be found accompanying hot does and could be anywhere within their entire range on a given day, often even bedding outside their core area. Unattached bucks roam around in search of hot does. Where competition is high, bucks routinely "herd" hot does away from high-activity areas to isolate them from other bucks.

93

Weather has a big influence on deer movement. Deer will move, for instance, in a light snowfall, but a snowstorm will subdue activity. Movement usually picks up again a couple of days after a big storm. Photo by Roman Jaskolski.

The "post-breeding period" begins around Thanksgiving and essentially continues until the bucks lose their antlers. Hunting season is closed in many parts of the country during much of this time. As breeding winds down, ritual rutting activity decreases and bucks soon begin to return to their core area. Movement is at a minimum unless a hot doe stirs them from their rest. Any does that didn't conceive during the peak breeding period recycle 28 days later, bringing on the "secondary" rut and its relatively minor buck activity. As the period progresses, food sources once again become more important.

Weather/moon phase

The weather and moon phase have a major influence on when and how much deer move. To maximize your time afield, you must understand how these factors affect deer movement. Let's examine some specific factors.

Temperature: Generally, colder temperatures cause deer to burn more calories for heat retention so they must feed longer and more frequently. Hot weather, on the other hand, tends to subdue activity and causes them to bed for longer periods. During warm weather, movement tends to be limited to the relatively cool early morning and late afternoon periods.

Rain/Moisture: Light rain, mist and, to a lesser extent, fog stimulate activity. This is because a deer's sense of smell is more acute in high-moisture conditions, perhaps giving him added confidence. Also, deer feel safer in the subdued light that accompanies these conditions.

Heavy rain causes deer to seek canopy cover, such as pine thickets, spruces, cedars, etc., where they will wait out the rain by either bedding or simply standing. Deer are usually active just prior to and after a rain.

Wind: High winds, especially when erratic, make deer nervous because the noise and movement created by the wind can't be separated from that of potential danger. Consequently, they often bed up and remain on the alert. Deer seem to feel at ease in steady light to moderate winds and will move in these conditions. Wind direction in itself is not a factor in deer movement, though certain wind directions tend to be associated with conditions that can influence movement.

During the rut-preparation period, which usually coincides with bow or early firearms season, bucks are on a predictable travel pattern from bedding to feeding areas. However, big mature bucks are often somewhat nocturnal. Guide Kirk Sharp (right) had to roust this early season Alberta buck from cover for Jim Gordon to get a shot. Photo by author.

Snow: A day or two prior to snow storms, deer movement can be high, but activity slows once the snow begins to fall in earnest. Contrary to what many think, activity is low immediately following a snowstorm but usually picks up on the second day after a storm has ended.

Cold Fronts: The sudden drop in temperatures with the arrival of a cold front nearly always triggers a major increase in deer movement. If the temperature falls far below normal for the region, deer movement may not hit full swing until temperatures moderate a little.

Moon Phase: All other factors being equal, deer activity on dark or new moon phases is highest during the early morning and late

Where hunters have the best access — roads, trails, cutlines, fencelines, edges, powerlines, etc. — expect hunting pressure to be highest. The deer know this and react accordingly. So will the wise big buck hunter. Photo by Bill Marchel.

evening hours. Minor movement may take place at midday and midnight. The opposite is true during the full moon phase – most movement is at midday and midnight and early morning and late evening movement is minimal.

Terrain types

Cover availability and terrain influence how and when deer move. In general, the more open the cover, the less the deer move during daylight hours. Conversely, the more extensive and heavier the cover, the more active deer are in the daytime. In relative terms, this is true regardless of hunting pressure, weather, etc.

Cover type and density can also have an impact. For example, bucks in heavily pressured areas of the Southeast have learned to seek out nearly impenetrable briar and low-brush jungles in cutovers (logged areas with regrowth). They literally have a maze of tunnels weaving through these cutovers, and for some deer, most daytime travel may take place within one large cutover.

The location of security cover also has a dramatic affect on travel patterns throughout the country. Every region has some form of security cover to which deer orient. Some examples are the standing cornfields of the Midwest, the lodgepole thickets of the Northwest, the spruce swamps of the Northeast or thick weed patches in the prairies of North Dakota. Deer use such areas as their home base.

Physical features such as fence lines, old logging roads, rivers, streams, strips of cover, thickets, open woods, swamps, hills, saddles and fields, to name a few, dictate where and how deer travel. Bottlenecks and funnels can really direct deer movement on a local basis and can be of huge importance to hunters.

Buck:doe deer ratios and density

Good buck/doe ratios (say, 1 buck per 3 does) create buck competition and, consequently, increased buck activity during the rut-related periods. Poor ratios (say, 1 buck per 10 does) decrease buck competition and result in a "softer" rut with less buck movement. Overall, bucks are more nocturnal and make less buck sign when the ratio is poor.

Higher deer densities mean bucks don't have to travel as far to find does. This can limit the daylight travel time of rutting bucks. On the other hand, high deer numbers usually mean increased competition for food, requiring that deer feed longer and more often.

Hunting pressure

I have saved perhaps the biggest influence on travel patterns to the end. In most parts of the country, hunting pressure impacts travel patterns more than any other single element.

Before we look at hunting pressure and nocturnal bucks, it is helpful to first learn how to pattern our fellow hunters. As a group, hunters are truly creatures of habit and tend to make similar choices given the same set of circumstances. This allows us to accurately predict how they will move about and hunt. Upon patterning hunters, we can then predict the travel patterns of deer reacting to them.

In identifying hunting pressure, there are certain assumptions about hunters we are safe to make. We know, for example, that opening day, the last day, holidays and Saturdays are peak pressure days in most places. We can also rest assured that hunters will descend upon the woods through popular and easy access points such as roads,

Most hunters think only distant and remote tangles of cover will harbor pressured bucks, but often, over-looked places right under the hunter's nose — such as abandoned homesites, grownup farmsteads, isolated clumps of cover, a thicket next to an interstate, the rough next to a golf course — provide undisturbed security for secretive bucks. Photo by Bill Kinney.

trails, cutlines, fence lines, edges, powerlines and trails. The areas closest to these access points get the most pressure and those the farthest away the least. With these assumptions, we can get a pretty good handle on the nature of most hunting pressure.

I often equate hunting pressure to pouring water over uneven terrain. Imagine water (hunting pressure) being poured over a central point (a favorite access location). As the water runs downhill, there is less and less water the farther it goes. And as the water seeks its lowest level, there are high-ground areas that get little or no water. Imagine that the bucks go to this high-ground, which is basically void of water (pressure). How far the water goes and how much high ground is left depends on the amount of water poured. These undisturbed high-ground areas are not necessarily the thickest, nastiest cover or terrain around because hunters often seek out such areas thinking that's where the deer will be. The high ground may be an isolated clump of brush, a thicket next to an interstate, a posted tract of property, the rough alongside a golf course, a weed patch in the middle of a field or anywhere hunters fail to check out. Of course, distance in itself is a type of high ground, as are physical barriers such as swamps, steep terrain, etc. Essentially, big bucks end up where they are least disturbed.

Bucks generally don't become nocturnal on opening day of bow season and remain that way until season ends. Instead, they react daily and weekly to the amount of pressure being applied, and their travel patterns are directly influenced by when that pressure takes place, and when it doesn't. We also know that where and how pressure is applied has a lot to do with where the bucks go, how they move and the types of security cover they choose.

THE FOUR PERIODS OF THE RUT

The Season In Overview

F OR MANY YEARS, I'VE PRESENTED SEMINARS on trophy hunting at various whitetail shows across North America, and no matter where I've been, one of the most popular subjects I've discussed has been "patterning bucks throughout the season." While giving my opening statement at a patterning seminar, I generally ask how many hunters in the audience ever take stands to wait in ambush for bucks. As you probably can imagine, practically every person in the room throws an arm into the air.

It's obvious that our skill in choosing the best locations for some type of ambush directly affects our success. Furthermore, that ability to choose a spot wisely is directly linked to understanding and predicting the travel patterns of bucks. To me, understanding these movement patterns and having the skill to predict them is the essence of whitetail hunting.

THE FOUR PERIODS OF THE RUT

In this analysis, we will follow and predict the changing travel patterns of a big buck throughout the season, with emphasis being placed on patterning, tendencies, habits, sign reading, etc. Obviously, such comprehensive coverage of this subject cannot be done properly without including the influences of the various phases of the rut. The entire hunting season (and even beyond) can be divided into four separate time frames, each with its own set of conditions that directly influence buck travel and behavior.

To be sure everyone's up to speed, we'll start with an overview discussion of these four periods of the rut and the most important

*This book covers a period of several months that begins with the rut-prepara-
tion period, which has a distinct beginning marked by the velvet-shedding
process. Velvet shedding often is helped along by rubbing, but primarily, it
simply "falls" off as it separates from the hardened antler.*
Photo by Bill Kinney.

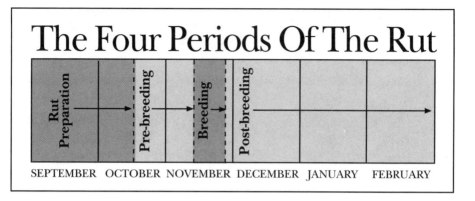

factors in each affecting travel patterns. What's important here is that we all understand that the different periods exist and that they each have effects on the deer we're hunting. In following chapters, we'll get into more details on each period.

The overall time frame being discussed here begins when bucks shed their velvet in late summer and ends when antler shedding takes place the following winter/spring. Within this window of time, four distinct periods exist, each distinguished by well-defined transitions in rut behavior and travel patterns. Obviously, these changeovers do not occur at the same dates in all parts of North America, and that presents a problem when writing to a geographically diverse audience. Fortunately, for the most part, these dates do coincide rather closely in states and provinces along the same general latitudes.

As we pass through the various periods, I will discuss dates, but they will vary somewhat depending on the locale. Generally, dates that mark certain important events, such as velvet shedding, breeding, antler casting, etc., are consistent within a state or province. Exceptions to this would include Mississippi, Louisiana, Florida, Alabama, Texas and a few other hot-weather states. In some of these places, the window for breeding (and thus, fawning) is not precise since the timing for maximum fawn survival is not as critical in the absence of severe winters. Also, many of these locations were restocked years ago with whitetails from several other geographic regions, and frequently, these pockets of deer have retained their old breeding dates.

For purposes of our discussion of the rut, I've selected an aver-

During the early part of the rut-preparation period, bucks are still hanging out in bachelor groups. They normally break up well before this period ends. Photo by Erwin & Peggy Bauer.

age of dates that would follow a latitude across North America just above an east-west center line of the U.S. As one moves farther south, these period changes are likely to occur later, and in regions farther north, they might begin slightly earlier. If in doubt as to when breeding occurs in your hunting area, check with a local wildlife biologist. State/provincial game agencies keep track of this type of management information and are happy to share it.

The rut-preparation period

This period most often begins the first week of September as bucks shed their velvet and spans approximately six weeks, ending sometime in mid-October. These dates are fairly consistent in all northern states but can extend into November in South Texas, Alabama, Mississippi, northern Mexico and other places with an exceptionally late breeding period.

The beginning point — velvet shedding — for the rut-preparation period is rather precise. Shortening daylength triggers the process by dictating the flow of hormones that control when velvet is shed. In any given herd, velvet shedding generally occurs over a 7 to

Scrape establishment and checking become the predominant buck rut activity during the pre-breeding period. Consequently, scrapes and scrape lines are the most important type of sign during this period for locating and predicting travel patterns. Photo by Erwin & Peggy Bauer.

10-day span.

The close of this period is more gradual, however, and not as easy to pinpoint. When the rut-preparation period draws to an end, there are no obvious physical changes in the bucks; the change is in their attitude, which involves a shifting of their primary interest from food to does.

After velvet shedding, bucks immediately begin preparing themselves for the upcoming breeding rituals by rubbing their antlers on trees and bushes. As a rule, they will rub trees over most of the routes they travel and quickly will form rub lines. These rubs will be used as the primary sign with which we will pattern bucks during this entire period.

The rut-preparation period is a difficult time of the year for relocating bucks. As we all know, bucks are most visible in July and August when their racks are still in velvet. Often, mature bucks can be seen in fields long before dark, and they appear to be uncon-

Throughout the breeding period, mature bucks are almost always found in the company of receptive does. Generally, the only time big bucks are seen alone is in their transition from one doe to another (which is usually at night) or when some disturbance has separated them from their doe. Photo by Erwin & Peggy Bauer.

cerned about being observed. But about the end of August or early September, these bucks disappear. They can be difficult to find again since they generally relocate to some degree and adapt new travel patterns.

Such a dramatic change occurs for a variety of reasons. First, the bucks have been putting on their winter supply of surplus fat and have been growing their antlers during the summer. Both require large amounts of high-quality food. By late August or early September, all antler growth has ended and sufficient body fat has been stored so that long hours of feeding in these prime fields no longer are required.

Also, the highest protein content and most desirable portion of a food plant are located at the tips while the plant is growing. By late summer, plants that had been tender and tasty have quit growing and become much less palatable overall. As a result, bucks normally shift over to browse and various other types of food found in the woods. During this period, rubs and rub lines provide valuable visual markers to help us find/relocate bucks that have gone to a "woods pattern."

The rut-preparation period is an excellent time in which to pattern and kill a particular buck since he generally is on a very predictable, regular pattern from bedding area to feeding area and back again. Scrapes will be established during this period, but most are "boundary" scrapes made at random and are not the primary sign used for patterning now.

The pre-breeding period

In most places, this second (and shorter) period of the rut begins around mid-October and ends three or four weeks later, usually around November 10. The period ending actually comes when the first does become receptive for mating (the beginning of the breeding period). In some southern states, the pre-breeding period can be later, with actual breeding beginning in mid-December or even January.

As noted, the start of the pre-breeding period is somewhat indistinct but essentially occurs when bucks shift their priority from food to does. Not surprisingly, this causes a change in travel patterns. Now, the building interest in does causes an escalation in scrape activity. With this change, we begin to rely primarily on scrapes and scrape lines to predict buck travel.

Like the rut-preparation period, movement patterns are again rather predictable, though not quite as reliable as before. Now, bucks establish regular circuits of scrape checking, instead of being on a strict bedding/feeding pattern, and the distance travelled changes dramatically. Whereas bucks in the rut-preparation period characteristically move one to three miles in a 24-hour period, now the daily range could jump to 10 to 15 miles, depending on the nature of the habitat, local buck:doe ratio and deer density. Still, the travel patterns of bucks are predictable, and they continue to center activity around their core areas.

When patterning a buck during this period, the hunter quickly realizes how critical an understanding of the concept of family units becomes. After all, the buck is now starting to seek out those doe

After the peak of rut, rest, recovery and seclusion are the top concerns of a big buck. They are apt to be very nocturnal during this period, except maybe for feeding and late breeding activities. Photo by Roman Jaskolski.

groups since they will be the focal point of his interest during the breeding period. We, too, must know where those family units live and how bucks will be accessing them. This is where our skills at reverse sign reading will pay dividends by helping us to see the "big picture" of travel patterns.

The breeding period

In nearly all states and provinces, this period is the shortest, at approximately 12 to 18 days. In northern regions, the first does become receptive around November 8 and the final breeding takes place near Thanksgiving. In central Canada, breeding might begin around November 11 and end about November 24. In South Texas, it might begin around December 14 and end just after Christmas.

Although the beginning and ending dates will vary from north to south, the length of the breeding period itself remains fairly constant everywhere, assuming the herd has an adequate number of breeding males to go around. If not, unbred does will continue to recycle at intervals of roughly 28 days. We'll look at this phenomenon in more detail a little later.

The beginning and ending points of the breeding period are the most sharply defined of all, especially in northern habitats. The period change generally occurs almost overnight. For example, there might be practically no does in heat in a certain area on November 8 and the big bucks are still unoccupied. On November 10, several females might become receptive and nearly all of the bigger, more dominant bucks will be in the company of "hot" does.

During the breeding period, the travel patterns of a buck change radically and we must change our hunting tactics radically as well. Rubs and scrapes no longer are valuable for predicting travel patterns of the bigger bucks. They now move along the patterns of the receptive does they happen to be with. Predicting the travel patterns of individual bucks becomes especially difficult. Consequently, this is not the best period to kill a particular buck, but it is a great time to kill a "random" trophy. The first two periods, when patterns are predictable, are much better times in which to set up on and take a certain buck. Overall, however, the breeding period is the time of greatest vulnerability for big bucks; no hunter should miss this opportunity.

During the breeding period, the best strategy is to hunt doe concentrations (family units), specifically the high-interaction areas. Now, you want to see as many does as possible, hoping the "right" buck will be traveling with one of them.

The post-breeding period

Once all does have completed their primary estrus cycle and the breeding period has ended, the fourth and final period begins. In most northern areas, this will start the first week of December and will be over when the bucks shed their antlers. As in previous periods, travel patterns are unique and hunting tactics definitely should be altered.

In most deer populations, only a very small percentage of females will not be bred in the first estrus cycle, barring severe buck:doe ratio problems. Often, these will be very young does (including 6-month-old fawns) or the odd mature does that have difficulty conceiving. These remaining unbred females will recycle 28 days later. So, for the first month or two after the primary breeding

This gigantic typical shed from Iowa scores 112! If the other side matched and with a 20-inch spread credit, the buck would have grossed over 240! The shedding of antlers marks the end of the time frame spanned in this book. Photo by author.

period, a small percentage of does will be recycling and bucks, at least some of them, will be on a rather unpredictable pattern as they seek them out.

When one of these late hot does turns up, bucks tend to concentrate on her for a couple of days until she's out of heat. Then, they once again disperse and search for other does. Hunting can be incredible when one of these breeding scenes is found, but they generally are difficult to locate because they're widely scattered and the buck concentration only lasts for a couple of days. Bucks also tend to be very reclusive and nocturnal during this period because of past hunting pressure and their rundown physical state from the rigors of the rut.

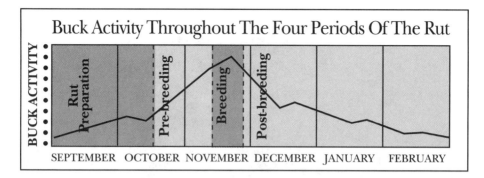

THIS GRAPH SHOWS THE RELEVANT ACTIVITY LEVELS of bucks in each of the four periods of the rut and an overall perspective of their activity pattern throughout the season. Its significance is the big picture, not the precise point where the line may be at any given instance.

As the title implies, this graph represents "buck activity," which includes rut and feeding activity. Consequently, the activity line begins September 1, at a baseline which represents mostly feeding activity. The increasing activity level throughout the rut-preparation period reflects a progressive rise in rut activity. The slight plateau in early October reflects what some refer to as the "pre-rut lull," which is a fairly short, low activity period just before rutting activity kicks off in earnest.

The activity line is on a steep, steady incline throughout the pre-breeding period. This reflects the accelerating scraping and doe-checking activities characterized by this period.

The activity line continues to rise during the breeding period to a high point that represents a narrow three to five-day window when the greatest percentage and number of does are in heat. This is the "peak of the rut," or the height of the breeding season. Activity immediately begins to fall as fewer and fewer receptive does come into estrus.

Buck activity rapidly falls during the post-breeding period as few receptive does are to be found, food and recovery become increasingly important and weather (especially in northern regions) and hunting pressure act to subdue activity.

A secondary rut begins 28 days after the primary one. The activity line once again mirrors a rise like that of the breeding period, except the activity level is substantially lower. This pattern is repeated in January and February, with each month reflecting a progressively lower level of buck activity. This is because fewer does are involved each month in breeding activity and a higher priority is placed on food and physical recovery. Eventually, buck activity level returns to its baseline level of feeding activity.

The primary variance in the pattern of buck activity depicted by this chart will be found in comparing colder northern latitudes to those in warmer southern regions. Late-born fawns are unlikely to survive in northern habitats, so secondary breeding activity is less predominant as one goes farther north. Also, poorer buck/doe ratios, regardless of the locale, tend to create higher rut activity levels during the post-breeding period — but a lower peak level — simply because there are more unbred does in the population after the breeding period has ended. However, the general trend of this buck activity pattern does not change dramatically throughout the whitetail's range.

Chapter 11

The Rut-Preparation Period

W E'RE ABOUT TO START FOLLOWING AND PREDICTING the travels of an individual trophy buck throughout the course of a hunting season. But first, let me make a few points about the specific animal we are patterning. We don't want to confuse the issue by getting side-tracked on all the possible movement and habit variations a buck might utilize. Instead, we'll select a single animal that will typify patterns of mature bucks.

Additionally, we will assume that the patterning discussion won't revolve around just any buck, but the biggest-racked buck in the area. Again, these patterns apply in a general sense to all bucks; however, the larger, more mature bucks do leave distinctive types of sign as opposed to smaller bucks. Besides, most of us want to take the largest buck possible.

One final assumption is that we already have located "our" big buck through the methods discussed in chapters 2 and 3. Whatever the source, we know specifically where he was seen or evidence of him was found. This is where we begin our patterning.

Getting started

From the hunter's perspective, one of the least realized changes in travel patterns is the dramatic increase in distance trav-

Food sources are one of the keys to patterning during the rut-preparation. Paul Chamblee shot this big Alberta buck late one afternoon over an agricultural food source. Photo by author.

eled by each buck as the season progresses. For example, a buck in early fall might range one to two miles as he travels from bedding to feeding and back again. That same buck's range could jump to 15 miles in a 24-hour period a month later as the rut escalates. Because of this, we must encompass a large geographical area, as much as 25 square miles, as we begin to learn certain features about the buck's entire range.

In the overall patterning process, we are going to be especially interested in two factors. First, we want to know the "head" and "tail" of his pattern, i.e., where he's coming from and going to. Once this has been determined, we will set up on the buck somewhere along that pattern, with the exact location depending largely upon the stage of the rut.

Secondly, we want to locate and define the buck's core area, the chunk of real estate where the buck spends up to 90 percent of his adult life. In that other 10 percent, his range will increase dra-

During the rut-preparation period, sparring matches are common, mostly as a means of reconfirming dominance ranking after the bachelor groups have broken up. This behavior also allows the bucks to learn how to use their rack and is a form of practice for the more serious fights that come later. Photo by Bill Kinney.

matically. The time of year our buck was seen has relevance to the location of his core area. If he was spotted not long after velvet shedding in early fall, for example, odds are great that he was in his core area. Whereas, a sighting during the breeding period might not indicate he was close to his "home."

Because we aren't certain a sighting indicates core area location and because we know his range will increase dramatically later in the season, we must select an overall area large enough to be sure we have encompassed his entire travel range (or as much of it as possible). In this regard, many hunters make the mistake of wearing blinders because they only have permission to hunt a certain 250 acres, let's say. Obviously, the buck's range is much larger, and we should be aware of certain features in a larger area if at all possible. For these reasons, I have chosen an area three by five miles, with the buck's one "known" location or sighting situated dead in the center.

I realize this is an extremely large area and that most of us will not have permission to hunt all of it. Still, the fact remains that our

This monster buck is rubbing a sapling in earnest. Rubbing is both a form of preparation for coming battles and a means of leaving visual and scent "signposts" for other deer. Rubs are the primary sign during the rut-preparation period. Photo by Bill Kinney.

buck travels a large area, and unless he encounters a game-proof fence or other major barriers, he doesn't pay much attention to property lines. But whether or not we have permission to hunt the buck's entire home range, certain features we can learn about the overall area will help us understand and predict his patterns in a way that will improve our chances of success.

By studying topographic maps and/or aerial photos, we can learn where roads and houses are and, more importantly, where they aren't. We can ride the roads and study the lay of the land. Where are the heaviest cover areas, the best feeding areas and the potential travel corridors? Where are the areas in which hunting is not allowed or is very limited? Where is the buck likely to go if hunting pressure becomes heavy? How does the location of security cover relate to where he wants to feed, his primary rutting areas and how his travel patterns may change? Many of these types of questions can be answered without having permission to hunt a buck's entire home

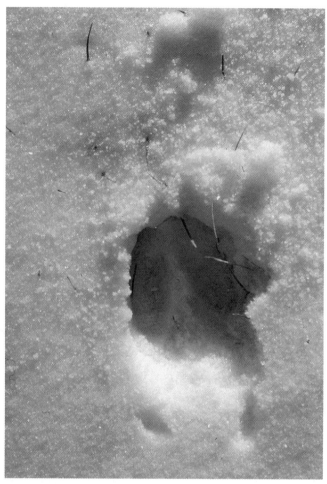

A big buck track in the snow — a classic type of deer sign. However, a big track doesn't necessarily guarantee a big rack on the deer that made it. Big tracks are most useful when they help confirm other sign. Photo by Bill Marchel.

range. It certainly helps to learn in advance as much background on your area's deer herd as possible to make accurate assessments of what's going on and why.

Rut-preparation feeding pattern

Again, our primary objective is to determine where our buck is coming from and going to. The most logical place to begin to answer that question is his destination. Early in the season, that will be where he's feeding. Scouting for the buck during the rut-preparation period must take into account his food preferences at this time of year. Let's assume it's alfalfa. Our objective will be to identify and scout as many of these particular fields as possible. Our first step in actual patterning can begin within a week after the bucks have shed their velvet.

During this period, the predominant sign used for locating and patterning will be rubs and rub lines. As described, when bucks come off their summer feeding frenzy, they go into what I call "the disappearing stage" because of changing food sources and body needs. Bucks that were visible every day in July and August now disappear into heavy cover and are difficult to relocate. Sign reading for relocating and patterning purposes now becomes very important.

Several types of sign imply "buck," though they don't always tell us much about antler size. Tracks often indicate larger bodied deer, which can give us a general impression of sex and age, but a large body frequently does not go hand in hand with a large rack. Some scrapes tend to be larger not because of the size of the deer, but rather from the amount of use. (This often is the result of visitations by many bucks, and they might or might not include our chosen target.) Other sign, such as droppings or beds, also might reflect body size but not necessarily antler quality.

Rub size — to be more precise, the diameter of the trees being rubbed — is generally our best indication of antler size (short of seeing the buck). This is certainly not an exact science, but big rubs usually point to big deer. Most of the larger/older bucks I've hunted, deer that would score 150 or more Boone and Crockett points, were working trees three to six inches in diameter at the height of the rubbing. This trait has been consistent enough for me to use it as a guideline in my own hunting. I've noticed that 1 1/2-year-old bucks tend to work finger-sized saplings, 2 1/2-year-olds characteristically rub trees 1/2 to 1 1/2 inches in diameter and young adults work trees from 1 1/2 to 3 1/2 inches in diameter.

As we begin the actual patterning process, we start by walking the edges of the food sources we have determined to be preferred. We also might scout the second choice feeding areas, if time and conditions permit. As we scout, we are interested primarily in the presence of rubs along the edges of the fields or browsing areas, and particularly in the diameter of the trees being rubbed. We can assume that the biggest bucks in an area usually will be responsible for the larger rubs.

After we've walked the edges of all of the preferred feeding areas we can find, we're likely to see that one or two of them have a lot more big rubs than any of the others. Here, we will make a big assumption — these big rubs belong to the buck we're trying to pattern, which means our first step of finding the buck is accomplished.

After finding his rubs, we now have to figure out where he's

119

going. Around the field, we find that the larger rubs aren't situated evenly around the field perimeter, but rather are concentrated near one corner, one end or along an edge. This also has special significance, because these areas of highest use indicate a direction of where the buck is coming from. For example, if the most active buck sign is along the south end of a field, then the buck is most likely bedding in that direction.

Certainly, there will be many trails leading into and out of the feeding areas where our buck's rubs are located. Again, the presence of larger rubs on certain trails will play a key role, this time in helping us determine which trails are being used by our buck. During the rut-preparation period, it's important to remember the buck is on a regular, predictable pattern between bedding and feeding areas. He generally has no reason to use a certain trail to enter the field one evening then switch to another the next. Instead, he tends to walk the same trails, like a bear coming to bait, unless he's significantly disturbed.

As a buck walks down a trail on his way to a field, for example, he rubs trees along the trail and he rubs them on the side of the tree he's facing as he approaches. A buck generally will not walk down a trail, turn in a semi-circle and rub a tree, then turn back around and head on down the trail again. Instead,
he forms a pattern of rubs facing away from the field when approaching and on the side facing the field when leaving. Obviously, different stands and set-ups would be required to hunt each trail. Trails that have trees rubbed on both sides usually imply that the buck is using the same trail to enter and leave the field. Again, a stand should be placed and hunted accordingly.

At this point, a more subjective aspect of patterning comes into play. Our goal is to determine where the buck is coming from and set up on him as near to his bedding area as possible, yet not let him hear, smell or otherwise know we're there. How far is far enough? If we set up 200 yards from the field's edge and the buck is coming from two miles away, we are not likely to see him. On the other hand, if he's bedded only 300 yards in from the edge, obviously we must set up nearer the field.

This is where we must use reverse sign reading to make certain pattern predictions based on tendencies, as we did with food prefer-

Three sizes of rubs — average, big and giant! The size of rubbed trees and the extent of damage are good, but not infallible, indicators of buck size. Look for something "big" for the area. Photos by author and Bill Marchel.

ences. By doing so, we do not have to rely on actual sign reading to determine where he's bedded and which trails he's using to get there. For example, trails that appear to travel in straight lines, going the shortest, most direct route between points A and B, are usually travel trails, implying bucks are going and coming from greater distances. They generally don't split off, meander or weave, as do browsing trails. Rubs located along these trails predict regular buck usage and distinguish them from other trails without rubs and probable buck travel.

Recognizing bedding areas

When trails begin to fragment and become fainter, and especially when littered with numerous droppings, odds are that they are entering a bedding area. Here, knowledge of bedding tendencies and travel characteristics must be applied to visible sign observation to predict bedding sites.

Bucks always prefer to bed on elevated sites when possible. When a ridge or hill is present, trails running along the bottom usually will be travel or feeding trails and will move parallel to the base. As bucks move upward to bed, the trails are vertical. Once trails become horizontal again, which is usually within the upper one-third of the ridgetop, we can predict we're in or at least very near the bedding area. The effects elevation changes have on buck patterns will be discussed in more detail in Chapter 19.

Often, bedding areas can be predicted by their mere location or the type of cover. Bucks always try to position themselves in unique locations that give them the advantage over intruders. They prefer to bed with their backs to the wind so they can see what they can't smell and smell what they can't see. On a ridge, they prefer to bed a short distance below the top on a point, shelf or bench that affords a panoramic view on what they can't smell. In such a location, the buck's back is to the wind so that any danger encountered from upwind allows an early escape. Seldom do bucks bed in low ravines (20 feet deep or deeper) because of swirling wind currents and because they are at a disadvantage in choosing escape routes. In elevated sites, bucks can disappear over the top and be out of sight quickly, but in ravines, they are relatively visible as they go up either side to escape.

Even in flat terrains, bucks use the wind/visibility combination to their advantage. In a small woodlot of five acres, with a wind blowing from north to south, bucks usually will bed on the south end, not in the middle. Normally, they will bed just inside the edge so they can see out of the brush but are difficult to see by anyone from the outside. If danger approaches from the downwind side, they can see it coming and escape out the other end. If danger is smelled from the upwind side where the bucks can't see, they can escape across the open, downwind side. For such reasons, bedded bucks in any of these situations are difficult to approach, and it's not an accident on their part that they choose such strategic bedding locations. Like food preference patterns, trail tendencies and bedding patterns can be learned, anticipated and predicted.

Once our buck has been patterned, using both predictable tendencies and sign reading, a stand or ambush is set up based on the travel pattern we've predicted. This is far better than simply hunting "good sign" in the manner many hunters do because we have kept the entirety of the buck's travel pattern in mind, rather than focusing too closely on any one piece of the puzzle. When hunting sign only without understanding the entire travel pattern, odds are high that we are not hunting the most productive location.

Travel Patterns In The Rut-Preparation Period

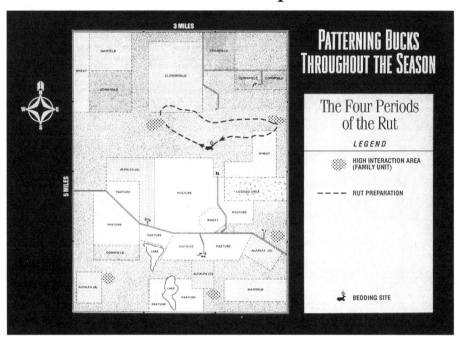

I N THIS AND THE FOLLOWING CHAPTERS, we'll use this map to provide a visual overview of our sample buck's hypothetical travel patterns throughout the season. To understand and predict travel patterns, we must examine a majority of a buck's range. Although we may not be able to hunt or access all of it, we must at least be able to identify the locations of critical destinations and elements, such as doe concentrations, food sources, travel corridors, preferred bedding areas, etc. We have arbitrarily chosen a 3x5-mile range for our buck's hypothetical pattern. A "typical" agricultural scene was chosen because it's a common terrain type across North America and lends itself to making illustrative points. As the periods are discussed, the travel routes in each respective period will be overlaid upon each other, as well the "typical" bedding sites for each period. The bedding site indicated on this map represents the heart of our buck's core area.

The rut-preparation period begins approximately September 1, at the time of velvet shedding. It continues for roughly 45 days, ending in Mid-October. Nearly all the functions in a deer's life are controlled through "photoperiodism," or the recording of short-ening day lengths through the eye. For this reason, we can accu-rately predict the time frames of the four different periods we'll be discussing.

Bucks during the rut-preparation period are more interested in food than does or rut activity. They are on a rather predictable travel pattern going back and forth from bedding to feeding. The buck's overall range, as well as the actual distances travelled, is rel-atively small and, in all likelihood, is the least of all the periods. The areas where bucks bed and hang out during the rut-prepara-tion period probably represent their true core area location, an important fact when deciphering travel patterns. Although not yet heavily involved in rut activity, bucks are actively engaged in rub-bing activity. The establishment of rub lines will be our key to locating and patterning bucks this time of the season.

Ultimately, when all factors are considered, the buck estab-lishes a travel route and living pattern that is logical, at least to him. Our sample buck is bedded reasonably close to food sources and his overall pattern is relatively short. Undoubtedly, much of his feeding activity is done at night since it only takes him a few minutes to travel the short distance from his bedding site to either field. On the way to the fields, he happens to pass through two high-interaction areas, but primarily because the does within them are also using the same food source. He is not yet interested in the family units, but that will soon change.

As expected, he's bedding and living within his core area. Only some special need for food or hunting pressure is likely to move him from this area. Rubs are apt to be found along his regu-lar lines of travel, with concentrations occurring near his bedding site and in the vicinity where his trails intersect the clover and wheat fields.

Chapter 12

The Pre-Breeding Period

WITHOUT A DOUBT, THE PRE-BREEDING PERIOD is my favorite time in which to hunt a specific big buck. Like the rut-preparation period that precedes it, the pre-breeding period features regular, predictable buck travel, but now, the odds are starting to swing toward the hunter because daytime activity is on the rise.

In most parts of North America, the pre-breeding period lasts three to four weeks. In more northern latitudes, it usually starts in early to mid-October and ends the first or second week of November. The pre-breeding period occurs approximately one month later in Mexico, South Texas and some other southern regions.

The establishment and maintenance of dominance rankings within a buck population is something of a year-round process, and the pre-breeding period sees a lot of interaction among males as they seek to gain a competitive edge on breeding rights. Every buck wants to be a breeder, and he does what he can to boost his opportunities in that regard. The pre-breeding period is a time of increasingly frenzied last minute preparation by the bucks, characterized by frequent sparring matches, widespread scraping activity and regular checking of family units. In short, the influences of the rut now affect travel patterns radically.

The beginning date of the pre-breeding period is not precise, at least as far as observed sign is concerned. Its beginning is predictable, however, to within a week or so. What is most significant now is the fact that the buck's priority has switched from food to does. He continues to feed, of course, but more of his time, thoughts

126

This mature buck is in the classic scrape-making posture, something frequently seen during the pre-breeding period. Here, he's working overhanging branches directly above the scrape. He often smells the branches to determine which other bucks have also visited the scrape and works his face over the branches to leave his signature scent to advertise his own presence. Scent is transferred primarily from the sides of the face, where it has been deposited by passing the face over the tarsal gland. It is also transferred from the preorbital and frontal glands (located on the face) and possibly even from saliva. Photo by Erwin & Peggy Bauer.

and travel are directed toward the opposite sex.

The reason the beginning date of the pre-breeding period is not so precisely defined is that this progression of priority from food to does takes place gradually over a span of 7 to 10 days. Physically, it is controlled by the decreasing daylength (photoperiodism). As the days grow shorter, the buck's system automatically gets a specified dose of the male hormone, testosterone, which is emitted into the bloodstream from the testicles. The amount of testosterone emitted increases each day during this transition period, so that each buck instinctively begins to place evermore priority on does.

Big, fresh scrapes get the hunter's adrenaline pumping. Such sign certainly implies that one or more bucks have recently been in the area, but the mere presence of a fresh scrape doesn't tell us what time of day a buck will return to check it or how close he's bedding to the scrape. Photo by Bill Marchel.

More miles to cover

Like the rut-preparation period, the pre-breeding period is characterized by predictable patterns of buck travel; however, important changes do occur. Where the buck is coming from, i.e., his bedding area, still might be the same as in the previous period, but where he's going most certainly will change. Before, he had been traveling regularly to some food source, but now, his objective is to check on does and his priority destination is probably going to be a high-interaction area within the range of a family unit. A prime food source most likely will be nearby (which is the reason the doe group is there anyway), and it might appear that the buck is there for food when he's really there for does.

In the earlier rut-preparation period, a buck's travels probably would not regularly take him to more than one or two family units. Now, however, his travels might carry him to a much greater number

Not all scrapes are located under overhanging branches, although most are. A well-used scrape lies alongside this rubbed fence post, which happens to be on a favorite buck crossing on the Mosquito Indian Reservation near Battleford, Saskatchewan. Photo by author.

of doe groups, with the exact number depending on the distance between family units and just how much time is left before some does will come into heat. Regardless of the number of family units being visited, though, the buck is certain to expand his overall travel distance dramatically from what it was only a few weeks or even days prior.

As a general guideline, I feel the average buck in the rut-preparation period travels one to two miles in a 24-hour period. Whereas, the same buck in the pre-breeding period will cover 8 to 10 miles daily if deer densities are high and as much as 15 to 20 miles if densities are extremely low. Obviously, with such a radical change in travel distance, our predictions of travel patterns also must change.

One final change in this period should be obvious. It's not hard to deduce that if the buck is traveling many extra miles, he has to spend more hours on his feet. The critical question is: how much of that distance is covered during daylight hours? The answer varies dramatically from area to area. Time of travel is very dependent on the buck:doe ratio, which influences the level of breeding competi-

This record Manitoba typical was taken by Carson Smith, a longtime friend and fellow hunter. We were both hunting this buck, Carson on one scrape line and me on another only a couple hundred yards away, when Carson shot him late one afternoon in 1984. Carson has killed many super bucks and is one of the best whitetail hunters I've ever known. Photo by author.

tion, and the amount of hunting pressure, which determines his degree of nocturnal travel. In either case, it's a safe assumption that all bucks are more excited about the prospects of breeding now and have a tendency to move earlier in the afternoons and remain active for longer periods in the mornings, making them more vulnerable to hunters.

Not only is there a dramatic change in travel from the first period to the second, but there is also a significant pattern change from the beginning of the pre-breeding period to its end. The amount of testosterone fed into the bloodstream continues to increase throughout this period, causing the buck's excitement level to rise as well. This, in turn, tends to cause the buck to move his bedding area progressively closer and closer to where the action is — the high-interaction areas. Eventually, the buck will actually start bedding within these areas, with that move coming during the last few days before breeding begins. Where we will hunt him must change accordingly.

Prime time for scrapes

The frequency of scrape checking also escalates toward the end of the pre-breeding period. Here, competition is a big factor. Bucks want to monitor the most active scrapes as often as possible because they sense a hot doe might choose a particular one at any given time. Whether the buck's scrape checking occurs at various times around the clock or is strictly confined to the dark hours will be affected by the amount of hunting pressure.

As bucks focus their attention on high-interaction areas and move their bedding areas closer, they drop off portions of their pattern in areas where doe activity is minimal or nonexistent. For this reason, early rubs and scrapes located farther from the family units often will be abandoned, causing that sign to go "dead." Without knowing the whereabouts of the other nearby family units and the stage of the rut that's currently underway, a hunter might get hung up on abandoned sign, only to realize too late that he has been hunting where the buck was, not where he is now. During the last 7 to 10 days before breeding begins, we must keep a constant eye on the sign being left at the high-interaction areas, as these locations certainly will influence his overall travel pattern.

During the rut-preparation period, rubs and rub lines were the predominant sign used to locate and pattern our buck. In the pre-breeding period, scrapes become more reliable as indicators of his travel pattern and predictors of his return to a specific place. A relatively small number of half-hearted scrapes likely were made during

131

As the pre-breeding period progresses, bucks begin paying more attention to does. They frequently monitor the does' progress toward breeding readiness through scent communication, as this buck is obviously doing by his trailing behavior. Photo by Roman Jaskolski.

the first period, but these were not serious enough to predict the buck's return. But during the pre-breeding period, the presence of more scrapes (and specifically, the establishment of scrape lines) is the visual cue that this period is in full swing. Scrapes and scrape lines are now the sign used to predict travel patterns.

As discussed, scrapes are established intentionally in locations where bucks expect does to find them. Therefore, a conscious effort is made to travel to locations frequented by family units. This is not necessarily the case with rubs, though rubs will continue to be made in these heavy scrape areas, as well as elsewhere on our buck's travel route. As we focus on the scrapes, we find there are different types that tell us something about the likelihood of a return and when that return might occur.

Defining scrape types

Technically, I don't feel there are really different kinds of scrapes in the sense that the average hunter could walk up and say, "Oh, this is a boundary scrape and that is a breeding-area scrape." In reality, all scrapes have a similar appearance when initiated. The real difference among them is where they are established. How much use they get usually will determine their eventual size.

I do classify scrapes into three categories based on their location rather than their appearance. This classification is worthwhile because there are some generalities to each group that tell us something about when/if bucks are likely to return.

The scrapes with the least promise are boundary scrapes. Normally, these tend to be noticed first in the early season, and they usually are associated with food sources and relatively open terrain. Many times they are located along the fringe of something — a field edge, hedgerow, fence line, narrow corridor of travel cover, the edge of islands of cover situated in open areas, etc. As a rule, most such scrapes are established and worked at night and thus are not great prospects for hunting. Their best value is to help us locate our buck, identify his food sources and assist in unraveling and predicting his overall pattern.

Trail scrapes are those found inside some type of cover and, as the name implies, usually are located in relation to some type of trail or system of trails. They are frequently visited during daylight hours and are good hunting bets, depending upon their precise location and how long it is until the breeding period starts. Their locations tend to define the travel pattern of bucks more than do those of any other scrape types.

A final type is what I call breeding-area scrapes, so named because of their location. These key scrapes are established and maintained within small, focused areas where the most interaction between does and bucks occurs. Here, odds are best that the "right" buck can get with the "right" doe at the necessary time. All other bucks in the area also know this, and scrape activity here is concentrated. Numerous traveling bucks target these tiny areas and key their activity around them. As a result, in some cases, trail scrapes become breeding-area scrapes simply from heavy use by a lot of bucks. They develop into large, well-used scrapes and truly are centers of activity for rut activity in the last portion of the pre-breeding period.

Putting it all together

Armed with this knowledge, it's time to predict some travel patterns of our buck within our three-by-five mile chunk of land. Just as we located him by the presence of big rubs and predicted his rut-preparation period movement pattern on the basis of rub lines and tendencies, we will do much the same in this period — except scrapes and scrape lines now will be the key sign.

Early on, the odds are good that our buck still will be bedding in the same core area as before, though his overall travel pattern now is much larger. As in the first period, we will scout the edges of the primary food sources, especially the No.1 preference for this time of season, to look for boundary scrapes along the edge of the feeding area. We can't be sure it is "our" buck making certain scrapes, but if scrapes are present where we found the large rubs in the first period, odds are good that the same buck is making them. Unless some external factor alters his living pattern, he will probably continue to bed in his core area for much of the pre-breeding periods, perhaps moving out temporarily toward the end. If we did not locate him in the rut-preparation period (which is the best time to identify his core area), the presence of big rubs — both old and new — will be the best evidence that the fresh scrapes belong to our buck.

Like in the first period, the buck has no reason to use a different trail each day. Some trails will have scrapes along them while others will not. Obviously, those with scrapes suggest use by our buck and perhaps by others.

As with the rub lines, we can learn a lot about his direction of travel from the scrapes, even if no identifiable tracks are present on the trails themselves. When a buck walks down a trail and stops to make a scrape, he paws the debris behind him. If the scrape debris has been pawed away from the feeding area, we can assume it's an entrance (afternoon) trail. If the debris has been thrown toward the field, it's a morning (exit) trail. Should it be pawed in both directions, of course, he might be using the same trail to both enter and exit the feeding area. Hopefully, we'll be able to find some tracks and rubs that help substantiate our ideas about what's happening.

Scrapes will help us determine where our buck is heading to and from. As in rub-line hunting, the real value of the scrapes is to help us unravel and predict his travel pattern. We do not want to

The author took this old Alberta buck several years ago at the end of the pre-breeding period by finding his fresh scrape line in a rut area. Photo by author.

hunt a scrape per se, but rather, his pattern and, specifically, a point along that travel route that affords us the best opportunity for a successful ambush.

As we follow trails toward the bedding area, we use the presence of scrapes and big rubs to tell us which routes to follow. Eventually, by using our knowledge of trails and bedding tendencies already discussed, we make an educated guess as to where he's bedding. We then set up on him accordingly.

Generally, our stand sites will be located closer to the bedding area near the beginning of the pre-breeding period and will move progressively toward the high-interaction areas or doe concentrations near its end. That's because when breeding begins, you can be sure that the big bucks won't be far away from the does.

Travel Patterns In The Pre-Breeding Period

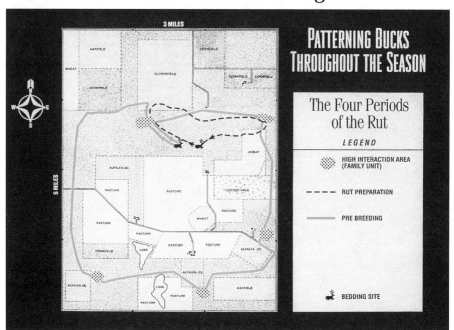

THE LENGTH OF THE PRE-BREEDING PERIOD is substantially shorter than the previous rut-preparation period. The period begins around mid-October and ends when the first wave of hot does hit the scene. This timing is intended to be general since we can't give specific dates for every region of North America. Except for some Deep South states, however, these dates are fairly accurate for most locales.

Because of shorter day lengths and, consequently, a greater emission of testosterone into the buck's bloodstream, he's now more interested in does and the breeding ritual than in food. That's not to say he gives up eating entirely; he certainly doesn't. But, this heightened interest in does alters his travel pattern. However, he's still on a regular, predictable pattern, but it's a different one from the previous period. Bedding, for the most part, still occurs within his core area.

His escalated interest in breeding has dictated a major change in both the length of his travels and where he goes. Instead of food sources being his destination as in the rut-preparation period, females have become top priority. Through scrape activity, he now effectively checks the condition of females and advertises his presence by visiting family units (doe concentrations) and especially the high-interaction areas (doe funnels). Here, he scent-marks rubs and scrapes to advertise his own presence in hopes of attracting a receptive doe. Scrape and scrape lines now become our primary sign to both locate and define his travel patterns.

Even though he's still bedding in his core area, his overall distance of travel, much of it done at night, increases dramatically. The high-interaction areas become his primary focus. Even at night, he's apt to use the safer travel corridors and natural funnels, such as the woods between the two lakes. He avoids houses, dogs, traffic or other places where human activity is high.

From a hunting standpoint, it's important to realize the increase in travel distance has taken place and that the more distant locations are likely to be visited at night. A hunter could be sitting over "fresh" scrapes down near the lakes that were worked at 2:00 a.m. This is just one of the reasons why it's critical to know a buck's core area and his overall travel pattern.

Chapter 13

The Breeding Period

O F THE FOUR SEGMENTS OF THE RUT, the breeding period is the shortest. But what it lacks in length, it more than makes up for in excitement, both for deer and those who hunt them. At no other time of the season does the average whitetail hunter stand such a good chance of seeing a big buck in a vulnerable position. Many of the greatest trophies are taken at this time.

The breeding period is not only the shortest period, it also has the most precise beginning and ending dates. In most areas, this period spans 15 to 18 days. The exact length is affected by the buck:doe ratio and the geographic location. The normal span is around 16 days, but it tends to become longer where there are far too many does per buck.

A period without a pattern?

Unlike travel patterns during the first two periods, movement by big bucks during the breeding period is erratic and less predictable. In the early fall, the buck himself determined where and when he wanted to travel. During the breeding period, however, while he is in the company of a doe (which is most of the time), his pattern is dictated primarily by her. The good news, from the hunter's perspective, is that the doe's pattern is fairly predictable. She continues to move from bedding to feeding and back again and

During the breeding period, big bucks often show up that are never seen during other times of the year. This remarkable buck was shot on the Kenedy Ranch in Texas. Note the forked G-2s and G-3s on both sides — very unusual in whitetails. Photo by author.

tends to be confined to her small core area. Her travels often lead a wary buck into vulnerable situations. The bad news is that we don't know which doe he may be with at any given time. Consequently, keeping tabs on a given buck during this period is difficult.

The pattern is there, but we cannot accurately predict it because the buck himself does not know what he's going to do. Generally, as the breeding period gets under way, he will check his scrapes until he finds a nearly receptive doe waiting in the vicinity. She might or might not be located within his core area, depending upon his dominance ranking and the amount of buck competition. In any case, he's likely to remain in her company and breed her periodically, assuming he can fend off challenges from other bucks, for one to four days. A doe's actual estrus time is about 24 hours, but this

139

Neck outstretched, head held low, short choppy strides — this is the classic rutting posture of an excited whitetail buck. A good-smelling doe is certain to have been nearby when Erwin and Peggy Bauer snapped this photo.

Hunting strategy during the breeding period is simple — hunt the doe groups. Where the does are, the bucks will show up. Photo by Troy Huffman.

additional "buffer" period probably is intended to allow adequate time for a dominant buck to find a receptive doe, thus assuring that superior males have adequate opportunity to do the lion's share of the breeding.

After she's been bred and goes out of heat, the pair might remain bedded together during the daytime; however, when they next begin moving around in the evening, the buck will leave her and travel to one or more high-interaction areas. He then works scrapes in breeding areas and physically checks the condition of many females. By morning, he's usually found another hot doe and repeats the tending and breeding cycle. For the most part, dominant bucks are seldom seen alone in daytime during the breeding period. The more balanced the buck:doe ratio, the more this statement holds true.

The older the buck, the more family units he'll likely visit, partly because he's been around long enough to have found more of them. A more equal buck:doe ratio also will cause more family units to be visited, and a higher deer density and/or the presence of more family units will shorten the average travel distance of the bucks. An

This buck has been caught in the act of "flehmening," which is a stereotypic behavior of hoofed mammals. Apparently, the "lip curl," as it is also known, is performed in an effort to analyze the condition of a possibly receptive doe. Photo by Erwin & Peggy Bauer.

unbalanced buck:doe ratio means more does per buck, making extensive buck travel less necessary. All of these factors add up to a very unpredictable buck travel pattern during this period.

I've always felt that the breeding period is a poor time to kill a specific buck. On the other hand, it's a great time to take big bucks at random. Even though buck travel patterns are unpredictable now, it's the time when big bucks make more mistakes and are more vulnerable than at any other time of the season. This is true because the buck is often out of his familiar core area and he's following the travel pattern of a doe. Plus, neither the buck nor the doe is nearly as cautious as they would be if traveling alone. The breeding period is that magical time when a big buck is seen in an open field at 9:30 in

The chase is over here. The doe is standing still for the buck and breeding is imminent. For a chance at this moment, a big buck will risk all. Photo by Roman Jaskolski.

the morning, when he's usually safely back in the timber before dawn. And, it's the time when a buck and doe are jumped along a sparsely wooded fenceline or from a tiny clump of brush in an open field. This is certainly the big buck's greatest period of vulnerability.

A little privacy, please

Earlier I noted that a buck with a doe now generally will be on her travel pattern, not his. We know this is true because we nearly always see the doe walking in front, followed by the buck. When she stops, he stops. If she turns left, he turns left. If she runs, he's usually on her heels. Normally, the receptive doe will continue to move on her ordinary course of travel within her core area. However, there are exceptions to this.

In many areas I've hunted where the buck:doe ratios are nearly equal and buck competition is high, I've seen bucks herd and isolate their does to areas generally devoid of deer. Many times, I've watched a buck work a doe in a fashion similar to that of a cutting horse working a cow. The buck moves back and forth to keep the

The breeding period is when most giant bucks are killed. Peter Swisteen shot this incredible 200 2/8-point typical during the peak of the rut in Saskatchewan. Photo by author.

144

doe from going into her traditional cover areas, where he knows there are other bucks waiting to steal her if they can.

In some areas, I've found a big buck and doe holed up as far as two to three miles from the other deer concentrations, and in unlikely locations where I'd never intentionally have looked for them. Of course, unless there's snow or you actually see them traveling into such a place, these unlikely hideouts are extremely tough to locate within the short window of time they are being used.

Timing is everything

In the previous two periods, we relied heavily on sign, particularly rub and scrape lines, in predicting our buck's travel patterns. The sign was physical evidence of where he had been, and it allowed us to make some predictions as to the likelihood of his return. In the breeding period, rubs are made and some scrapes are worked but they do not reliably indicate a return of the buck. Rubs and scrapes now are made or worked according to where a buck happens to be at a particular time, which is greatly influenced by the movements of the receptive doe he's with. For all practical purposes, rubs and scrapes now are of little benefit to us in our efforts to predict travel patterns, especially for more dominant bucks. Their greatest value is simply to show us there are bucks in the area.

Understanding the difference in travel patterns from the pre-breeding period to the breeding period is critical. Mistakes are more commonly made by hunters in their approach now than at any other point in the season. Scrapes and rubs are very visible types of buck sign, and hunters rely heavily on both. Scrapes and rubs become even more visible late in the pre-breeding period, and certain travel patterns become most obvious at this time. Many hunters have just "figured out" a certain buck when the scrapes suddenly go dead and the rubs grow dull, and generally, the buck doesn't show himself. The problem is made even more complex by the fact that the hunter presumes the buck has become nocturnal (which he might well have) because he isn't seen. Yet, the scrapes are freshened daily. So, the hunter continues to sit over his scrape line, seeing only small bucks and presuming the big boy is there but nocturnal.

Generally, when a big buck picks up the first doe off his scrape line, he does not check it with any regularity in daylight hours during

145

the rest of the breeding period. Instead, the more subordinate bucks that do not have does regularly check these scrapes without fear of the more dominant animal. To the casual hunter, it appears such scrapes are being worked regularly by the same buck. This is a case in which sign reading alone with not do the trick. We must know both the beginning and ending dates of this period.

Sign of the times

Some types of sign are valuable during this period, but they are not the traditional types for which most hunters look. Running tracks, large and small together, are a good indication that heavy buck:doe interaction is taking place. This usually means the presence of a hot doe and is valuable in locating bucks and breeding activity. But, this type of sign needs to be fresh, and it must be hunted as soon as it's found. Rutting activity often will move elsewhere once that particular doe is no longer receptive.

Another valuable type of sign during this period is the buck "travel" trail used to get from one family unit to another. I first got onto this back in the mid-'80s in Manitoba while hunting a particular buck in a low density area. Fortunately, there was good tracking snow, and as I followed various sets of buck tracks, I soon saw a pattern emerging. There were favorite, loosely defined trails with only buck tracks connecting the various doe concentrations over a rather large area. Only after I realized that these trails led to other family units did their course make any sense to me. Finally, I could see that there was a well-defined network of connecting trails bucks used to travel between family units. The bucks didn't always walk the same trails, but there were similar movement patterns that utilized the best cover and most direct route to get from Point A to Point B. I soon learned that bottlenecks and cutlines (rights-of-ways or other cleared strips) that intersected these travel corridors were great ambush sites, especially during midday.

As we refer back to our "model" buck, we realize that during the breeding period there are some aspects of his travel pattern we can predict and others we can't. For example, we can be sure he'll be visiting many of the family units in his travel range and that he'll be following the movement pattern of specific does within those concentrations. We know he'll use some of the travel trails between family units, and odds are good he'll favor those family units closest to his core area. We also can safely assume that he will abandon some of his previously used haunts (many of which contain numerous rubs and scrapes) and concentrate his activity in the vicinity of family units — specifically, the high-interaction areas. But, the predictability of exactly where the buck will show up at any given time certainly is reduced from what we might have found earlier in the fall.

Generally, my entire hunting time during the breeding period is spent hunting family units and buck travel trails. Which doe concentrations I hunt on a particular day is affected by the number and freshness of big buck tracks I find, as well as the presence of running tracks or any other type of sign that indicates breeding activity is taking place in a given location. If there is snow, tiny, dull-red spots sometimes can be seen on a hot doe's trail, as she drips secretions from the vaginal area. Also, yellow-brown droplets of urine/gland secretions can be found along the track of a really excited buck, as he dribbles this secretion on the snow from his tarsal (hock) glands. By pressing this substance between the fingers, we often can detect that pungent "buck" aroma that verifies we're onto something.

In summary, the breeding period is a great time to kill a gigantic buck, but in order to do so consistently, the hunter must understand and recognize that different tactics are required. Still, when it all comes together, a hunt during "the peak of the rut" can be marked by plenty of buck sightings and excitement. The fact that most true trophy whitetails are taken in the breeding period just goes to show how vulnerable mature bucks are during this special time of the season.

Travel Patterns In The Breeding Period

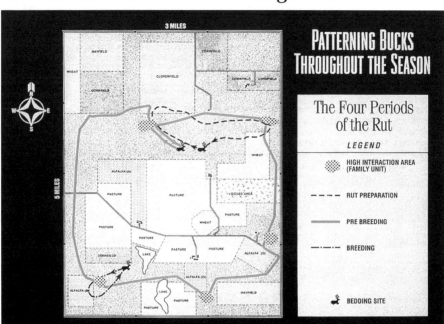

O F THE FOUR PERIODS, the breeding period is the shortest in duration. In a scant two weeks or even less, breeding in the first estrus cycle is pretty much over. In most central to northern latitudes, an accurate starting date would be from November 6 to 10. The period ends in most northern regions a day or two prior to Thanksgiving, or around November 22. Farther to the south, the breeding period is generally later. The South Texas rut, for example, is nearly a month later, with peak breeding activity beginning around December 14 and ending around Christmas.

During this period, bucks are totally preoccupied with does, specifically those receptive for breeding. Their travel pattern now becomes totally unpredictable, as they are subject to be found anywhere within their range. Such sign as rubs and scrapes, which were vital in the two previous periods, are now virtually useless to us for predicting travel patterns, especially for the more dominant, mature bucks. Now, the does become the key "sign," as most buck activity is dictated by the location and activities of does within the family units.

Essentially, a buck travels from one family unit (high-interaction area) to another until he finds a receptive doe and a situation where his dominance level will allow him to retain possession of her. If the buck competition level is high, he is likely to "herd" her to a spot where other bucks seldom travel to keep her isolated for a couple of days until she goes out of heat. In other cases, the doe may remain on her short pattern within her respective family unit, dictating the pattern of travel while the buck follows.

The sample buck on our map has found a receptive doe outside his core area and will remain with her until she ends her estrus cycle or until a more dominant buck takes possession. You can see from the short travel pattern that he's apparently following her as she dictates the pattern. A day or two later, he virtually could be at any other point on our map with another doe. During this period, he doesn't have a great allegiance to his core area as he'll take a hot doe anywhere he can find one. Buck activity and vulnerability are at their highest now, but predictability is out the window and at its lowest!

Chapter 14

The Post-Breeding Period

M ANY WHITETAIL HUNTERS WOULD CLAIM the post-breeding period is the toughest time to catch a big buck with his guard down. Due to a variety of factors, not the least of which is the effects of hunting pressure, mature bucks are indeed a special challenge in the late season. However, that doesn't mean hunting after the peak of the rut is a waste of time; it simply means we once again have to adjust our strategy.

Beginning and ending

Like the breeding period, the post-breeding period has a distinct beginning date. Certainly that date will vary from one region to another, but it begins at roughly the same time each year in each specific locale. The period obviously picks up where the breeding period leaves off, beginning when the last wave of does ends their primary estrus period. In many northern latitudes, this date will fall between November 25 and December 1, but in some southern areas, it will be considerably later.

While the end of the primary breeding period obviously marks the beginning of this period, it doesn't mean there are no unbred does left at that time. There will be some. When these unbred does recycle some 28 days later, they will trigger what is commonly known

During the post-breeding period, bucks can become very nocturnal, making forced movement the best game in town. Larry Raveling of Iowa shot this 282-point non-typical on a deer drive. This buck may well be the largest non-typical ever to have been documented as positively killed by a hunter. Photo by author.

as the "secondary" rut, which will last approximately the same length as the first rut but is of less significance and intensity.

As we discussed in Chapter 7, out-of-balance sex ratios are a common reason does recycle, but even in herds with good buck:doe ratios, some does will be bred outside of the peak rut period. Some simply fail to conceive, for whatever reason. Often, yearlings and even doe fawns, particularly in areas with good nutrition, come into heat for the first time in late season, and they join the unbred older females in attracting bucks. Depending on the dynamics of the herd, this can result in a noticeable flurry of late breeding, enough to constitute a huntable pattern.

The post-breeding period ends at the time bucks shed their antlers. Thus, the length of this period varies greatly, as breeding activity and antler-shedding dates differ from one geographic region

The rut takes a toll on big bucks, and by the time the post-breeding period rolls around, the bucks are worn and haggard and spend much of their time resting in their core area. Photo by Troy Huffman.

to another. For example, the breeding period in northwestern Montana runs from around November 12 to December 1, which means any unbred does should be recycling between December 10 and 29. Bucks there begin shedding their antlers around January 1, which means the post-breeding period is limited to roughly one month.

On the other hand, the breeding period in South Texas runs from approximately December 14 to January 1, which means unbred does should recycle from January 11 through 29. Yet, many bucks in that region don't shed their antlers until late March, approximately two months beyond the beginning of the secondary rut, meaning the post-breeding period runs approximately three months.

The early days

During the post-breeding period, bucks tend to be especially nocturnal and reclusive, but in part of the period at least, they're willing to travel great distances in search of any remaining hot does. If we analyze the dates, we realize that there are few receptive does at the beginning of this period. For example, if the breeding period runs from November 12 to December 1, any unbred does would recycle 28 days later, meaning the first ones would become receptive around December 10. So, for more than a week in early December, there probably will be few hot does available. Of course, the big buck we've been following all fall doesn't know this, and he continues to roam from one family unit to another in search of unbred does.

During this early portion of the post-breeding period, buck travel patterns are somewhat different from those in the latter portion. Because there are few available does during this "gap" at the start of the period, buck travel is extensive. Bucks that had been spending a couple of days or so with each hot doe now are unable to find any, so they cover a lot of ground in their uninterrupted searching.

From a patterning and hunting standpoint, this early portion of the post-breeding period is a good time to take a big buck, at least relative to the rest of the period. In some regards, it's similar to the two weeks just prior to the breeding period in that bucks are covering large areas and focusing on high-interaction areas and family units. Ambush setups within or adjacent to these high-activity areas can pay off as bucks search frantically for any remaining mates. The biggest difference is that weeks of hunting pressure have made all deer more careful about moving in the open during daylight hours.

The secondary rut

After the first couple of weeks of the post-breeding period have passed, the travel patterns change somewhat. Now, the odd doe once more has become receptive, and breeding activity in these "pockets" becomes intense. Just as at the beginning of the breeding period, the doe selects a scrape regularly visited by the buck of her choice, basing her assessment of his status on the scent he has deposited there. But now, because there are many bucks constantly searching for the few does still available, buck competition becomes especially intense. (In this scenario, we're assuming a healthy buck:doe ratio, so relatively speaking, there is a very small percentage of recycling does available.) Again, there is an "announcement" period of a couple of days, in which the smell of the doe will alert any passing buck that she is approaching estrus. Bucks thus will often begin to congregate before she's actually ready to breed. Buck competition can be fierce and fights frequent, as bucks are drawn in from a large area.

Years ago, I witnessed such a scene in the Rio Grande region of Mexico in late January. Much of the terrain in South Texas and Mexico is flat, but I had leased a ranch that did have some fairly high hills, one of which overlooked a beautiful flat nearly a mile wide. I was running a commercial hunt on the property, and my clients and I had hunted the area off and on for a couple of weeks, but we'd seen few bucks there. Then, one day at lunch a hunter told me he'd seen a good buck in the flat that morning. We went back to check it out for the afternoon.

After situating ourselves in a strategic lookout position, we finally spotted a group of deer. As it turned out, there were 11 bucks and one tiny doe on the scene, and what followed was a floor show that lasted for two days.

From our lofty perch, we were fortunate to witness a rare phenomenon in the whitetail world. It was a classic display of dominance, as one big 8-pointer with a huge body maintained "possession" of the doe while other near-equal bucks fought, aggressively rubbed the brush with their antlers and constantly established and worked scrapes. A big 11-point buck with a 22-inch spread was second in line. He actually had a larger rack than the 8-pointer but was younger and probably weighed 50 pounds less. He would come close to challenging the 8-pointer but always backed down at the last minute.

All of this activity took place within an area no larger than 100 yards in diameter. Bucks on the low end of the dominance scale occasionally would leave, and new ones would show up. As each new buck came on the scene, the fighting and threatening again would erupt. We finally took the two largest bucks. At the end of the three days, the doe was no longer in heat and all remaining bucks disappeared from the area. Only by witnessing that scene from a unique vantage point for an extended period could I understand what happens during the post-breeding period.

One of the most significant lessons from that experience was the relevant unimportance of sign, primarily rubs and scrapes. There was very little buck sign in that area before the doe became receptive. The bucks congregated in that particular location only because

During a late-season hunt in South Texas, the author finally shot this 170-class typical after hunting him for several days. The buck was very nocturnal and showed little interest in does. His end came when he stepped into an oat patch at last light. Photo by Gary Machen.

the doe happened to live there. Of course, there was a great deal of buck sign visible within a small area after the first day the bucks gathered, but I would have had to be extremely lucky to find that group of deer strictly on the basis of sign. The lesson is that these isolated breeding groups are not likely to be found by searching for concentrated sign.

The buck movement, however, was visible. Had I been on ground level in or near the area of activity, I'd have probably seen one or more of those 11 bucks moving around. Knowing that during

As the post-breeding period progresses, the bucks once again return to a feeding pattern, but much of their movement is likely to be at night or in low-light conditions. Photo by Bill Marchel.

much of this post-breeding period many of the bucks will have found such isolated hot does and that the majority of their time will be spent at such a scene, I've learned to pay special attention to any buck — large or small — sighted during this period. I also pay close attention to what he's doing. Does he appear to be traveling, or is he involved in some type of rutting activity? Pay particular attention to bucks with their nose to the ground. I'm always looking for any tip-off that an isolated breeding scene is nearby.

If a buck is seen exhibiting suspicious behavior, then a quick look around the area usually will show whether or not something's going on. If the breeding scene has been there for at least a day or so, visible sign should be present, such as running tracks, an abnormal number of buck tracks, signs of fighting (circular areas of scuff marks and tracks), an abnormal number of fresh rubs and scrapes, etc.

Once such an area has been found and it has been determined that breeding is still in progress, it's important not to run the doe from the area while hunting. Bucks might get spooked occasionally, but they will be reluctant to leave as long as the doe stays put. Hunting will be most productive by watching the fringe of the activity area and allowing the various bucks on the scene to show themselves. In all likelihood, the biggest buck present will be with the doe and following her wherever she goes. A second hunting strategy would be to try to anticipate where the doe is feeding or traveling to and set up an ambush en route.

Also, hunting such a scene means we must hunt close to the deer because time will be very short. At most, we might have only a couple of days of activity remaining. There's little way to forecast how much longer it will last, so we're forced to press the issue somewhat.

Changing priorities…again

Patterning individual bucks during this period is again a difficult proposition, much as in the breeding period. One significant difference is the use of a buck's core area. As you'll recall from the previous chapter, our big buck's core area wasn't utilized to any great degree during the breeding period. However, because so few does are actually receptive in the post-breeding period, he once again moves into his core area for bedding, then travels to various family units in search of does. Now that the height of breeding has passed, a buck's thoughts return more to food, security and survival. Consequently, he generally becomes more nocturnal and difficult to see. Sign is not as important now, as much of what's in the woods was put there prior to the breeding period. Knowing the boundaries of a buck's core area becomes particularly important now. As he focuses more on food, an ambush can be set up within the core area, keying in on the most prime food sources.

Because bucks are still searching in earnest for hot does, the high-interaction areas near the best available food sources will be visited frequently as bucks work the most promising scrapes in the area. Hunting there should still be productive.

Regardless of the region, these spurts of breeding activity progressively subside throughout the period. Each week, the importance of food, rest and security become more important while rut activity proportionately decreases. Within two to four weeks from the beginning of the period, bucks are primarily focused on feeding activity, security and physical recovery. The net effect is that they become very nocturnal and reduce their travel distance to a range more comparable to the rut-preparation period. The bigger bucks are especially rundown from the strenuous rigors of the breeding and fighting and now spend a disproportionate amount of time bedded.

Hopefully, we won't find ourselves still hoping to get a shot at "our" big buck during this challenging part of the season. If our scouting and hunting have been done properly, we'd like to think he already will be wearing our tag before the post-breeding period hits! If not, however, don't give up on taking a mature whitetail just because the prime period for buck activity has passed. Many great deer have been taken during the post-breeding period, especially by devoted hunters who refuse to give up. If the cards are played correctly, a late season hunt can pay "big" dividends. Yes, luck is always a factor, but it's up to us to enhance that luck as much as possible.

Travel Patterns In The Post-Breeding Period

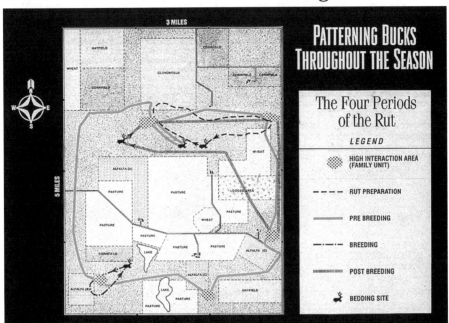

T HE POST-BREEDING PERIOD begins with the close of the breeding period and ends when the antlers have dropped. Around Thanksgiving in most parts of the country (later in southern zones), breeding activity gives way to more subdued buck activity, a greater interest in food and increased nocturnal tendencies. As this period progresses, buck patterns become more predictable, except for isolated breeding scenes.

Any does not getting bred in the primary breeding period will recycle 28 days later, causing flurries of rut activity, the level depending upon the buck/doe ratio and the region of the country. These extended breeding cycles are less common in northern regions because a relatively narrow window of breeding is demanded for fawn survival. This is not the case in more southern areas, however, as two to four breeding cycles are not uncommon since the fawn-survival window is wider.

Rubs and scrapes become more important for patterning than in the previous period but will never be as valuable as during the first two periods. Bucks tend to once again bed in their core area.

159

From a hunting standpoint, it's often difficult to locate these isolated breeding scenes because they appear and disappear within a matter of two to four days. When they are discovered, action can be exciting because bucks tend to congregate and activity is high as several bucks vie for the right to breed.

On the map, the travel pattern of our sample buck points out that he has once again established his bedding routine within his core area. His travel distance is greater than in the rut-preparation period but not as great as in either of the other two periods. He still visits family units, though mostly at night, hoping to find any recycling does, but his eagerness is less now than in the pre-breeding period.

This period may extend into late January, February or even March, depending upon when antlers are shed. Obviously, the farther from the peak breeding and rut activity, the more dramatically overall buck movement decreases. As one moves in either direction away from the breeding period, buck travel patterns become more subdued; food interest becomes higher; bucks are more nocturnal and travel patterns are shorter and more predictable.

BUCK PATTERNS IN DIFFERENT HABITATS

Chapter 15

Patterning Prairie Bucks

W E'VE SEEN JUST HOW STRONG AN INFLUENCE the various parts of the rut have on our big buck, and hopefully, this has pointed out the necessity of varying our hunting strategy throughout the season. We've also examined the tremendous impact hunting pressure can have on the buck's movement patterns. But, our look into the life of mature bucks would not be complete without a detailed discussion of the ways in which the habitat affects their lifestyle. This is the final piece of the patterning puzzle.

The fact that the whitetail is native to an enormous variety of habitat types, from the dense evergreen forests of Canada to the steamy plains of South America, bears out how amazingly adaptable this animal is. We don't know for certain how many of the 30 original subspecies still exist. Haphazard restockings in this century and habitat destruction throughout the Americas have muddied that water. However, we do know that today's whitetail is found from timberline to sea level, and this ability to make a living in a wide range of habitats has only added to his mystique.

While the whitetail occupies a vast number of habitats, I believe that from a hunting perspective only four categories are significant: prairie, woodlot, wilderness and fringe. In addition to those, another

In the wide, open spaces of eastern Wyoming, the author shot this heavy, 185-class non-typical during an early season "push." Photo by author.

physical factor — elevation changes — also is worth a close look. Certainly, the rise and fall of the land uniquely affect how and why bucks move.

The four distinct habitat types differ primarily in the way in which they influence travel patterns, not necessarily because they usually look so different. In some cases, they do have an appearance all their own. But from a hunter's viewpoint, their real uniqueness

lies in the relation-
ship between bed-
ding and feeding
areas; travel routes
between these areas;
where deer seek
sanctuaries under
pressure and other
factors affected by
the features of the
environment. In this
and the next four
chapters, we'll drop
the big buck we've
been patterning into
a variety of habitat
and terrain situations
to see how his pat-
terns might be affect-
ed by the physical
surroundings.

*The true prairie habitat starts just east of the
Rockies. Whitetails are competing with mulies in
much of the open country of the West and are living
in places that seem more suitable for antelope than
whitetails. Photo by Neal & Mary Jane Mishler.*

What is prairie habitat?

Prairies happen
to be one of the
more visually distinct
habitats because of
their overall lack of
cover. The term
"prairie," as used here, does not necessarily mean Western antelope
country. Rather, it applies to any habitat so devoid of cover that deer
often bed in virtually open expanses, or in very confined patches of
cover. Certainly, antelope country that holds whitetails falls under
this heading, but prairie habitat is more than that. Nearly every state
and province has some region or localized areas I would place in this
category.

For example, a lot of the Eastern Seaboard states have vast

stretches of farmland with little cover. Often, deer live in this open country exclusively. Parts of Texas have mile after mile of actual prairie sliced with deep, rough canyons. The Corn Belt of the Midwest typically has huge expanses of cultivated fields, as do a number of Canadian provinces.

Various other states have literally millions of acres, with or without agriculture, that fit into the category of classic "prairie" country. Such places as Washington, Wyoming, Montana, Colorado, Idaho, Alberta, Saskatchewan, Manitoba and others have large areas of wide-open, plains-type habitat, both with and without creek and river bottoms offering some small slivers of cover. The distinction between prairie and woodlot habitat is the former's lack of significant timber or "bush" for bedding, as well as a unique travel pattern wherein deer, especially bucks, utilize the open spaces for security when pressured.

Travel patterns

When deciphering and predicting travel patterns, we should be especially concerned with locating bedding and feeding areas since they are among the buck's main destinations. Thus, the identification of these areas forms the foundation of any type of successful ambush strategy.

Pinpointing bedding and feeding locations might seem simple enough on the surface. However, each is apt to change throughout the hunting season because of the influences of the changing periods of the rut, varying degrees of hunting pressure and seasonal shifts in food sources. As we'll see, understanding how these changes affect deer movement in various types of habitat and terrain gives us some insight into what to expect throughout the season without having to decipher such patterns simply from sign reading and/or visual observation. With this "reverse" approach, sign reading and observation of deer are used to substantiate travel patterns already suspected.

In the rut-preparation period, our prairie buck would surely be utilizing a favorite early season food source, such as soybeans, with a short and regular travel pattern from bedding to feeding and back again. Every region has food sources preferred by deer during different periods of the year, and prairie habitats are no exception.

165

It's hard to believe that cover-loving whitetails can adapt to the seemingly bleak prairies, but the author's big Wyoming buck proves the prairies are now home to the whitetail. Photo by author.

Generally, this changing preference is very predictable from one year to the next, which can be a huge advantage in predicting when and in what way the buck's pattern will shift. An example might be soybeans in the early season, followed by a freshly cut wheat field, then a freshly cut corn field and finally alfalfa in the late season.

By the pre-breeding period, the buck's range will have increased to include several food sources and favorite scrape areas — not because of the food itself, but because each of these food sources usually has a family unit of does and their dependent offspring living nearby. Again, bucks are very familiar with the locations of these family units within their travel ranges.

During the breeding period, the big buck is likely to spend most of his time paired up with various receptive does around one of the prime feeding grounds, such as an alfalfa field. Throughout this period, he will be on a random daily travel pattern, moving as far

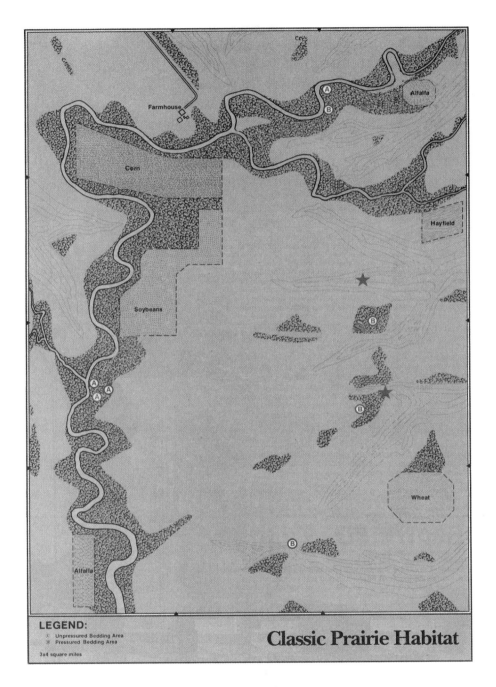

LEGEND:
ⓐ Unpressured Bedding Area
ⓑ Pressured Bedding Area

3x4 square miles

Classic Prairie Habitat

and as often as needed to satisfy his urge to breed. Once he's finished with a doe, he will be off to check for more in the vicinity.

In the post-breeding period, the buck again will return to his core area to seek security, placing somewhat more emphasis on food.

Giant bucks do indeed live in prairie habitat. Frank Pleshac shot this 252 1/8-point non-typical in the classic prairie country of eastern Montana in 1968. Photo by author.

During this time, he might or might not cut down on the size of his travel pattern. Most likely, he'll still check some scrapes, but not as many or as often as during the pre-breeding period. He is also likely to seek out heavier security cover for bedding.

How does hunting pressure figure to affect this buck's pattern in a prairie habitat? As in other environments, we naturally would expect him to become more nocturnal in his movements and to spend a higher percentage of his time in security cover. Also, one of the most unique and predictable characteristics of prairie bucks is that even the least disturbance in the relatively small cover pockets immediately will send them packing for wide-open country. This might seem stupid on their part, but it really isn't. Big whitetails are often much harder to hunt out on the "prairie" than in the thicker cover that typically lines waterways or other fertile ground.

Many prairie bucks will spend the majority of the year down in the thicker bottoms, but they're quick to take a hint that hunters are around. Disturbances from such things as pheasant or other small game hunting, deer scouting, etc. will spook bucks in early season. Many will immediately seek bedding locations entirely away from the cover for the duration of deer season. A likely exception might be during the breeding period when a buck simply cannot resist the temptation to bed with his hot doe.

No matter what the habitat type, bucks everywhere have some locations they consider to be true sanctuaries. In the case of prairie habitat, this often takes the form of completely open surroundings. Here, bucks effectively become much like pronghorns, depending heavily on their vision; however, unlike pronghorns, they rarely roam much during daylight hours. Usually, a mature whitetail buck will seek out a clump of tall weeds, a weedy fence line, a rockpile, a depression or ditch in a field, rough canyons, rocky drainages with sparse vegetation, sloughs or other inconspicuous cover.

In prairie habitat with no stream or river-bottom cover, bucks will adopt a travel pattern much like the one described above regardless of pressure. More pressure will simply cause such bucks to become completely nocturnal. Less pressure will allow a hunter to at least see one traveling across the open terrain on occasion. An absence of agriculture will make patterning much more difficult since natural food sources will have to be identified and located. Often, these foraging areas are not as concentrated as we might wish for hunting purposes.

In prairie habitats, deer densities tend to be much lower than elsewhere. The result is that bucks as a rule travel much farther in search of receptive does. And in open country, a spooked buck thinks nothing about running four to five miles before bedding again. Thus, when hunting such habitat, we must think of travel patterns in a much larger sense than usual.

Hunting tactics

As you might have guessed by now, prairie habitats can at times be frustrating to hunt. Often, bucks that have been observed at long range with binoculars or a spotting scope can't be approached to within shooting range before they spook and head for the next county. At other times, because the open terrain is so vast, bucks holding tight can't even be located and jumped from their beds by drives or still-hunting.

One of the first steps in figuring out a prairie buck is to identify and locate his food sources, if possible. Trails bearing large tracks in or adjacent to field edges will verify bucks are in the area and that such a location is at least one of their food sources. Trails leading into and away from the food source at least should give a general direction to head in your search for the bedding area. If some bushes, shrubs or trees are anywhere near the food source, rubs and scrapes should be visible as further verification.

In classic prairie habitat, bucks can be hunted rather traditionally, as long as they are bedded in the obvious cover along the rivers or streams. Scrape hunting, rattling, deer drives and treestand and ground ambushes all can be effective when utilized properly. But, extreme caution must be used to avoid spooking prairie bucks from their beds, as they will quickly abandon such cover. It's usually best to hunt the edge unless the cover is large enough to allow an interior setup without alerting bedded bucks.

During the rut-preparation period, a stand location should be closer to the bedding site, but again, we must be careful not to make the buck aware of our presence. Ambush points in open terrain are very tricky to approach without letting the buck spot us. Of course, it's no accident that bucks choose bedding sites that give them this visual advantage.

In the event no standard bedding cover exists or bucks already have moved to the open spaces to avoid hunters, a more innovative tactic must be utilized. If the bucks are not completely nocturnal, long-range surveillance with binoculars or a spotting scope during prime movement periods often reveals some portion of a travel pattern that allows for a later ambush. At other times, I've walked all day, following whatever sparse sign was available, in hopes of jumping a buck close enough for a reasonable shot. That strategy has worked occasionally. If you're lucky enough to get a decent tracking snow, fresh tracks might also lead directly to where a big buck is laid up.

The most important key to hunting such bucks is first understanding their travel pattern. Once that's accomplished (and it's no small feat), we have to trust our instincts and experience to decide on ambush locations. We must use the rut and its changing periods to our advantage, anticipating what our buck is going to do. Hunting pressure occasionally can turn out to help us, if we understand escape routes the buck might use to get away from other hunters. You can be sure the buck has worked to gain a home-court advantage in this kind of habitat, and to get a crack at him, we'll have to do the same.

Chapter 16

Patterning
Woodlot Bucks

W HEN MANY THINK OF A DEER HUNTING SCENE, they envision woodlot habitat. It's one of the most common and productive whitetail environments ... and has turned out some of the greatest bucks
of all time.

Woodlot habitat is really nothing more than your basic farmland with its a mixtures of various types of crop fields and patches of
timber, brush, logged regrowth and/or other types of cover. This
habitat typically contains a lot of human activity, including farming,
small game hunting, fishing, wood cutting, etc. And, there are plenty
of homes and roads scattered throughout most such places, bringing
heavy vehicle traffic. As a result, most woodlot deer are accustomed
to humans and understand their ways.

The percentage of cover in woodlot habitat varies a great deal.
It might account for as little as 10 percent of the total land area or as
much as 90 percent. If more than 90 percent is open, the area would
fall under our previous definition of prairie habitat, because bucks
frequently would be bedding in the open spaces. On the other hand,
if 90 percent or more is in cover, it more than likely would fall into
the category of fringe habitat, primarily because of the behavioral

Woodlot habitat is most often (but not always) associated with farmland, whether actively tilled or not. This scene is typical, with an old farm out building in the background and deer on a highly preferred food source. Photo by Bill Kinney.

patterns of the bucks. The most common woodlot mix is 50 percent or less cover, which accounts for most of the "average" farmland habitat in North America today.

Woodlot patterns

As compared to prairie habitat, the key distinguishing factor for woodlot habitat is that bucks here primarily bed in the cover throughout hunting season, as opposed to seeking the open terrain when under pressure. Woodlot habitat differs from a fringe-type because in the latter feeding and bedding locations are rather predictable, whereas in the former, neither bedding nor feeding locations are predictable (at least, not in a specific sense). Sure, the deer are feeding in one of the fields and bedding in one of the woodlots, but which ones?

Nearly without exception, all states and provinces have an abundance of woodlot habitat. In some Midwest, Northeast and Southeast states, a large majority of the habitat fits into this category. Almost

The Midwest is most often associated with woodlot habitat, but the truth is that this type of habitat exists throughout North America. Still, the Midwest is rightfully known for its corn fields, woodlots and giant bucks, as this 231-point, Minnesota non-typical killed by James Rath will attest.
Photo by author.

Patches of cover surrounded by fields and openings constitute "typical" wood-lot habitat. This photo points out preferred bedding sites chosen by big bucks. They like to bed on the downwind end of the woodlot where they can smell danger upwind and see danger downwind. The wind direction is indicated by the arrowed line. Photo by author.

anywhere there's farming, ranching and agriculture, there's woodlot habitat.

In most cases, the open portion of the habitat will have at least some agriculture. However, this isn't always the case. As an example, consider the Kenedy Ranch in South Texas, which I've hunted. It has woodlot types of cover in the form of oak motts interspersed among open, grassy flats. Although the flats are natural, deer feed in them rather predictably, and likewise predictably bed in the oak motts. Therefore, their travel patterns are similar to those of bucks in any other woodlot habitats.

Let's put our big buck into a typical woodlot habitat to see what type of travel pattern he might develop during the various stages of the rut. For purposes of this illustration, let's assume that we have an area that includes a "patchwork" of houses, roads, crop fields and cover, the latter being in the form of woods and logged-over areas of regrowth.

This near-book buck came from central Canada's farmbelt, a region of classic woodlot habitat. Photo by author.

As always, when trying to predict a buck's travel patterns, we must determine his destinations. These "wheres" change often in woodlot habitat, which is the main reason patterning bucks here can be so difficult. Such factors as changing food sources, shifts in the attitude of bucks from food to does (and finally, back to food again) and the amount of hunting pressure all directly affect where a buck travels. These changes occur in every habitat, but they're especially difficult to keep track of in woodlot country because a buck has so many alternatives for bedding and feeding.

In order to track our woodlot buck's bedding and movement patterns throughout the season, let's begin with his travel pattern under light to moderate hunting pressure. In the rut-preparation period after velvet shedding and before heavy scrape-line establish-

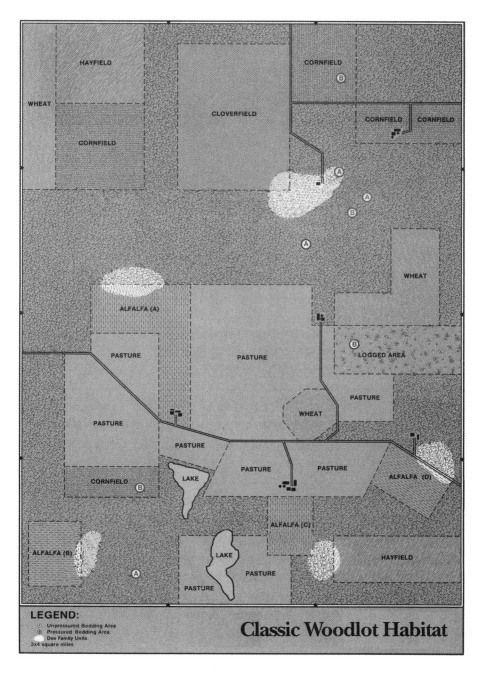

Classic Woodlot Habitat

LEGEND:
- Ⓐ Unpressured Bedding Area
- Ⓑ Pressured Bedding Area
- Doe Family Units
- 3x4 square miles

ment, the buck selects a typical bedding site located in the largest tract of cover in the area. For sake of illustration, let's say his preferred food source at this time is a clover field within his core area.

Typically, during the rut-preparation period, a mature buck

177

tends to utilize only one or two primary food sources (which almost always are located within his core area) and his travel pattern is predictable. The distance between bedding and feeding areas usually is short, and his core area almost always includes the home range of at least one family unit. As an example, let's assume the big buck we're following is using an old, abandoned house site as a staging area before entering the clover field each afternoon.

During the pre-breeding period, the buck moves his bedding site closer to his most promising line of scrapes. As we've seen, bedding areas likely won't change overnight, but rather, they move progressively as the buck anticipates the arrival of the breeding period. While the buck's shift in bedding locations between the rut-preparation and pre-breeding periods will not be drastic, we can count on his daily range increasing considerably. Now, the buck starts making full swings that encompass several miles and visits to multiple family groups.

Scrapes will be established and worked at each of these doe-concentration areas, with very little other scrape activity occurring between these sites. Nearly all of the scrape activity (at least, from our big, mature buck) will be at night, except possibly for that occurring at the first family unit he visits after leaving his bedding site. In his case, that probably would be near the clover field. Other bucks on a similarly expanded travel pattern also will be opening and working scrapes within the ranges of the various family units, causing some popular scrapes to become extremely large from repeated use. As you'll probably remember from our earlier discussion of rut sign, I call these "breeding-area" scrapes. They are hotspots to hunt during the last couple of weeks prior to the beginning of the breeding period.

When the breeding period actually starts, the buck moves his bedding site so that he can maintain contact with a family unit containing at least one receptive doe. Of course, in woodlot habitat, this is likely to be fairly close to a prime food source, such as alfalfa. Generally, the most dominant buck in a given location will maintain breeding control over the first doe to reach estrus in his core area. Bucks that rank below the most dominant one will seek and control other does as they become ready to breed. Where buck:doe ratios are good, several of the lower-ranking bucks in an area might be

Standing corn fields serve as security cover in the Midwest and other farm regions. These corn fields are difficult to hunt because movement within the fields is rather random and visibility is limited, as can be seen in this unique photo. Photo by Bill Marchel.

unable to find receptive does in their core areas, so they travel to other family units, hoping to find a different situation and available does. Quite often, even the most dominant bucks must seek does at other family units, especially at the beginning and end of the breeding period. As discussed in Chapter 13, the randomness of this movement is what makes a specific buck so hard to catch up to during this so-called "peak of the rut."

During the post-breeding period, the buck is run down from heavy breeding activity and spooky from the cumulative effects of an extensive hunting season. Consequently, he seeks heavier cover for bedding and reduces the size of his travel pattern somewhat. Breeding is still on his mind, but now, he doesn't exert nearly as much energy in scraping and breeding activity. His focus begins a noticeable shift from sex to food and security.

This giant is known as the "Illinois Road Kill" and is considered by many to be one of the most impressive bucks in the world. However, the score, which is only 176 3/8 typical because of a forked G-2, doesn't reflect the true size of the "basic" 8-pointer. Photo by author.

Pressured buck patterns

Now, let's look at the same buck going through the same hunting season and periods of the rut, but this time, under heavy hunting pressure. As we've noted, every habitat type has its own and sometimes unique forms of sanctuaries, at least in the mind of the buck. In the case of prairie habitat, as we saw, security is often found in the open spaces. In woodlots, by contrast, it's usually cover of some sort. Common types of sanctuary cover in woodlot habitats are standing corn fields (especially popular in early season throughout the Corn Belt of the Midwest); large thickets of any type; weed fields; cattail swamps; parks; subdivisions; acreage within city limits; farmers' back yards and any kind of dense regrowth following logging or other land clearing.

For all practical purposes, the travel patterns of this pressured buck are actually little different from those of lighter pressure —

with two exceptions: (1) the bedding areas often will be dramatically relocated; and (2) his travel most likely will be done entirely at night.

Whether a woodlot buck will choose to stay in the obvious cover or abandon it for a hiding place in more open surroundings usually depends on the size and density of the cover in his home range and how much pressure is being exerted on him. For example, in the rut-preparation period, if our buck is being bowhunted heavily by stand-hunters but is not being spooked from his bed, he'd probably stick with his preferred bedding site but would be almost entirely nocturnal.

By the time the pre-breeding period has rolled around, however, we probably could assume that the buck has been jumped from his bed one too many times. He might then opt to take advantage of a common type of security cover like a nearby field of standing corn. As many hunters know, hunting nocturnal bucks in standing corn is usually an exercise in frustration. The only real solution I know is to pay the farmer to pick his corn early!

During the breeding period, you might figure that even under heavy hunting pressure the buck would be quite vulnerable. This is true to some degree. However, we must remember that at this time he will be with a receptive doe more often than not, and these does will have reacted in their own way to hunting pressure. The disturbance of guns being fired and hunters tramping through the woodlots and fields is often too much for does. So, they also seek the same types of sanctuary cover as do the bucks. That could mean that both the buck and his doe could be hiding out in standing corn or a similarly difficult type of cover to hunt.

In the post-breeding period, the buck will seek sanctuary wherever he can find it, perhaps in a logged-over area thick with regrowth. His choice will have been forced upon him, partly because every one of the standing corn fields in the area now has been harvested.

Regardless of the amount of hunting pressure, the size of a buck's travel pattern in a woodlot habitat decreases as deer densities increase and as buck:doe ratios become more out of balance. An unbalanced sex ratio is, as we have seen, most often associated with heavy hunting pressure, and with such pressure, the average age of bucks in the herd declines.

181

Hunting tactics

Although woodlot habitat can be difficult to hunt, especially in areas subjected to heavy pressure, it offers hunters some advantages over other types of habitat. In prairie, wilderness and fringe habitats, locating the bedding area of a pressured buck, especially in his sanctuary cover, can be a major obstacle. In woodlot habitat, bedding areas might not be easy to find but the job is not as difficult as in the other types of cover. But in woodlot habitat, the big problem we often do face is deciding which bedding areas and/or food sources the buck is using.

As discussed, I prefer to hunt rub lines in the rut-preparation period and scrapes in the pre-breeding period. This follows the natural progression of our buck's travel pattern in early season. I generally rely on ambush setups, most often using treestands to give me an edge in visibility.

Like pressured bucks in any other environment, those in woodlot habitat can be exasperating to hunt. Because there are no elevated vantage points in standing corn fields and the vegetation usually is too thick to offer the hunter any real visibility from ground level, ambushes of any type are difficult. We must either use forced movement or hope the buck will exit the field under the low-light conditions of dawn or dusk.

As we know, unpredictability makes hunting a particular buck during the breeding period a shot-in-the-dark proposition, but more really big bucks are caught in the open during daylight hours now than at any other time. Our hunting time obviously should be concentrated near the family units and whatever cover connects their favorite areas.

With few exceptions, tactics for hunting woodlot bucks during the post-breeding period must involve relocating a nocturnal buck. If the pressure has not been extreme, he likely will return to his core area of early season and to a preferred bedding site within that area. Should the pressure be too heavy, however, he'll seek out whatever suitable sanctuary cover is nearest his core area.

The hunter spending a majority of his hunting time pursuing a mature buck in woodlot habitat soon learns that he's dealing with a streetwise whitetail. This deer somehow knows whether or not a barking dog means danger. How and where a vehicle stops as it passes down the road immediately tells the buck whether or not there's cause for alarm. (He somehow seems to recognize the difference between a farm truck and a hunting vehicle.) In other words, he usually knows whether or not he's being hunted. And when he knows you're after him, a mature buck can become nearly unkillable by legal means.

Chapter 17

Patterning Wilderness Bucks

THE WORD "WILDERNESS" SPARKS A VISION OF PRISTINE COUNTRY with no houses, roads, people, dogs or other signs of civilization. Most true wildernesses today are in the western U.S., western Canada and parts of eastern Canada, but there are some scattered elsewhere. A number of these have good whitetail herds while others don't.

The list of "classic" wilderness habitats with huntable populations would include western Montana; much of Idaho; northeastern Washington; northern portions of Minnesota, Wisconsin and Michigan; northern Maine; parts of Quebec, Ontario, Nova Scotia and New Brunswick; northern portions of Manitoba, Saskatchewan and Alberta; and much of British Columbia. Of course, this isn't to say that these areas are without any human impact. Logging, oil exploration and extraction, mining, trapping, fishing and other activities do occur, along with hunting. But, the overall flavor of these places is one of unspoiled backcountry.

For our purposes, however, "wilderness" will encompass a broad range of habitat types. Any area that has extensive cover without agriculture, or an area large enough that deer living there never actually utilize agriculture, meets my own definition of "wilderness" from a whitetail hunter's perspective.

With this definition, we quickly realize that many regions other than those named above can meet the criteria. For example, a number of Southern states have huge, timbered tracts (some logged-over, others not) in which deer never see agriculture. Parts of Texas, especially the East Texas Pineywoods region and portions of the South Texas Brush Country, also feature huge expanses of cropless timber or brush. Even the Mid-Atlantic and Northeast have substantial acreages on which no agriculture exists. Of all major whitetail

Because wilderness bucks often lead a life with little interference from man, they tend to move freely during daylight hours. Photo by Bill Marchel.

regions, the Midwest and the Great Plains have perhaps the smallest percentage of its land in this category due to widespread farming.

Many areas across the continent feature large tracts of timbered land with agriculture along their edges. Some deer live a number of miles inside the timber but occasionally come to the fields to feed, especially during periods of seasonal stress. These deer are living in wilderness habitat, but because they visit agriculture as part of their travel patterns, we'll include them in our discussion of fringe habitat in the next chapter.

General travel patterns

Many hunters who frequent wilderness habitat find whitetail travel patterns vague and confusing. The reason is that these hunters never actually identify critical areas and destinations used by deer. The animals don't wander aimlessly, even where cover is extensive. Rather, they have well-defined types of bedding cover, feeding areas and rut centers. These must be identified in order to pattern bucks properly in any wilderness habitat.

For example, deer in the vast, evergreen forests of western Montana generally feed along the edges of creeks, sloughs and swamps where snowberry and Sarvisberry bushes are plentiful. Whitetails on this feeding routine (most common from October through April) often bed in lodgepole thickets and on timbered ridges and benches. These habits are so predictable that they can be considered huntable patterns. Trails between the two types of areas usually are well marked from heavy use.

If you could remove all cover from the wilderness habitat except the concentrated food sources and primary bedding areas, you would have something that looks much like typical woodlot habitat. Wilderness bucks move in predictable patterns, but the continuous cover makes unraveling those patterns more difficult.

In wilderness habitats, water generally plays a bigger than normal role in the establishment of travel patterns. Often, preferred food sources and/or bedding cover are more abundant near water. Creeks, rivers and swamps usually are surrounded by higher ground, often causing deer to feed low and bed high.

Regardless of the area, there will be a changing list of preferred foods throughout the season. In much of the eastern half of the U.S., browse along the fringe of wet areas and openings comprises much of the early season food supply. In the fall, various types of acorns, fruits and other mast become favorites as soon as they hit the ground. Food sources are apt to change again in late fall and winter, depending on snow depth and availability in general. The point is that even wilderness habitats have a food pattern that changes in a predictable sequence each year.

Bedding area cover types also are identifiable and predictable. In the wilderness areas of western Canada, deer prefer bedding sites near the tops of small knolls and ridges that have some type of underbrush. They always prefer some elevation when available and often bed on benches along the sides of ravines when true hills and ridges aren't present.

Cover types can help in patterning bedding preferences. In the wilderness mountain areas of North Carolina, Tennessee, Georgia, Kentucky, etc., deer often seek out evergreen mountain laurel for bedding, especially when pressured. Dense cedar and other conifer thickets serve the same purpose in the Northeast. Understanding bedding preferences in a given region will help predict much of the pattern.

Carson Smith rattled in this book-class buck in wilderness habitat. Low hunting pressure, which usually means a balanced buck:doe ratio and a good buck age structure, sets the stage for rattling success in wilderness habitats. Photo by author.

Another important element involving food sources is the location of the doe groups. Because there are specific feeding areas in wilderness habitat, the concept of family units also applies here. Say, for instance, a preferred food is the small willow and other shrub browse growing along the edge of small, wet sloughs. These "potholes" or "meadow-swamps" are very common in most of the northern U.S. and in Canada and are preferred feeding areas. Consequently, small groups of related does and their offspring concentrate here, and these sites become hubs of activity (breeding areas) during the rut. Concentrations of rubs and scrapes usually can be found around the edges of these sloughs.

Wilderness habitats lack the big agricultural food sources, but openings are important nonetheless. The "edge effect" and the browse associated with small openings in big woods settings attract wilderness deer and often become focal points for feeding and rutting activity. Photo by Roman Jaskolski.

Patterns during the four periods

As in the previous two chapters, let's drop our mature buck into a typical wilderness habitat, then track his travel patterns throughout the four periods of the rut, both under light to moderate hunting pressure and under heavy pressure. First, we'll look at light pressure.

In the rut-preparation period, we find our buck living in a core area near a swamp and some prime lowland food sources. We find that he's bedding near the top of a timbered ridge in a central location between the security cover of the swamp and his primary food source. (His preferences in regard to elevation will be discussed in more detail in Chapter 19 when we address mountainous terrain.)

The buck's travel pattern now revolves around bedding high and feeding low. The typical pattern is for him to drop down to browse along the edges of several meadow-sloughs then feed along the edge of the swamp on his way back to his bedding site. Because he's not yet searching for does, his travel pattern remains short, predictable and targets food sources. Of course, this is just what we saw happening during the early fall in the prairie and woodlot habitats. It's just that there now is more cover for the buck, making his pattern harder to unravel.

In the pre-breeding period, our buck's primary interest has shifted from food to does and his travel pattern reflects that change. Sometime during this period, his bedding site will be moved closer to his most promising line of scrapes located near at least one family unit lying within his home range. A buck usually spends the majority of his time during this period near scrapes located in the "most popular" family unit in his core area. You usually can count on him checking those scrapes before he makes his longer circuit to more distant family units.

Our buck begins his scrape making/checking foray from his bedding area in late afternoon or early evening, then continues on to a number of others before finally returning to his bedding site. This often is a very long circuit, some of which will be done at night, but in contrast to other habitat types, deer here are less nocturnal because of the security of heavy cover. Daytime scrape checking is common.

Such a long pattern is more common in wilderness habitats because of lower deer densities and more buck competition for breeding rights. Lower overall hunter densities usually mean reduced harvest rates, and that keeps buck:doe ratios more balanced, as a rule, than in more accessible types of areas.

During the breeding period, the buck will once again be spending most of his time with a receptive doe from one of the family units he's been checking on. As elsewhere during this time, his travel pattern will be quite short while he's occupied with a female. Once he leaves her, he travels only far enough to find the next receptive doe. Every time he pairs up with a doe, he adopts her relatively short and predictable travel pattern between feeding and bedding.

In the post-breeding period, the buck has moved to a bedding site on the other side of the swamp. His travel pattern is substantially shorter, as he visits only a few nearby family units then passes through the swamp back to his bedding site. Interest has shifted

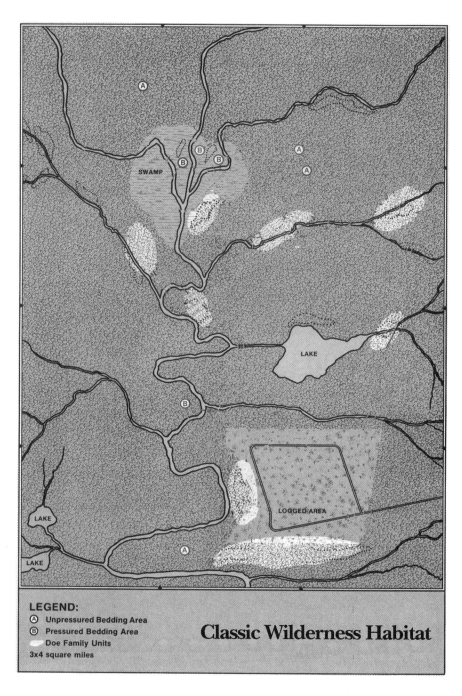

Classic Wilderness Habitat

LEGEND:
Ⓐ Unpressured Bedding Area
Ⓑ Pressured Bedding Area
⬭ Doe Family Units
3x4 square miles

somewhat more to food and security.

The travel pattern of the same buck under heavy hunting pressure probably wouldn't change much, especially regarding where he goes and the distances traveled. Of course, if pressure is really heavy, he will change his bedding sites and the timing of his movement as we've discussed elsewhere. Fortunately, in wilderness habitat, unlike most of the other types, extensive cover and a lack of concentrated hunting pressure mean we can hunt the buck somewhat harder ourselves before he seeks security areas and becomes entirely nocturnal. In the big woods, a buck spooked from his bedding site might settle back into the same area several times before finally deciding to seek an area with greater privacy. The extensive cover provides him with a greater feeling of safety.

But make no mistake: Heavy pressure can and will force bucks into security areas, regardless of the cover type. Such sanctuaries do exist in wilderness habitats, and they are well known to the bucks, if not to the hunters. By and large, they are places where people prefer not to hunt because of noise, distance, treacherous walking conditions, etc.

Common security types in the Southeast include swamps with low humps of dry land in them; pine and cedar thickets; logged-over areas with heavy regrowth; cane and briar thickets; and brush tangles caused by logging. Northwestern types include lodgepole thickets; very steep hillsides with benches; swamps; ridgetops and hilltops with heavy underbrush; willow thickets; and low evergreen stands. In South Texas or the adjacent Rio Grande region of Mexico, it's often large, dense thickets of whitebrush or blackbrush.

Outside the breeding period, we might find that the pressured buck has moved his bedding site where he's spending his daylight hours to some humps in a large swamp. An undetected approach to him would be nearly impossible in such a situation, and he usually will have several escape routes available. The rest of his travel pattern will likely continue to look much like his route under light pressure, and the extent of nocturnal movement will be determined by the amount of pressure in his core area.

In the breeding period, our buck and the doe he's with on any given day probably would react to heavy pressure by moving their bedding site to a dense cedar swamp or other especially nasty cover within the doe's core area. Because the buck is following her travel pattern, he's less likely to be nocturnal unless she feels pressured to that point.

191

Even without agriculture as a food base, wilderness bucks can obtain incredible size, as these two typical Montana bucks prove. The buck on the left, killed by Kent Petry, scores 198. Thomas Dellwo shot the awesome 199 3/8-point 6x6 on the right. Photo by author.

Hunting tactics

Being able to predict the travel patterns of a true wilderness buck requires that we have a thorough understanding of his feeding and bedding habits and how the geography affects his living patterns. Not to be overlooked is our need to be intimately familiar with the lay of the land. This, frankly, is work many hunters aren't prepared to do.

In wilderness habitat, as elsewhere, the buck's travel pattern will be rather predictable during the rut-preparation and pre-breeding period. But here, as opposed to what we might find in more open habitats, we will have less of a chance to pinpoint the deer through observation since visibility in wilderness habitat can be limited. This is especially true before the leaves fall in autumn, which generally occurs prior to the breeding period. Thus, our ability to find and read sign will be especially important. Once we've zeroed in on the buck's routes, traditional treestand and other ambush tactics would be our best bet. If I had to tell you a single trail to hunt during this time, it would be the one used by the buck as he leaves his bedding site. Of course, the nearer it gets to the actual breeding period, the more active the buck is likely to be, and the farther from "home" we might expect to be able to catch him in daytime.

During the breeding period, as you might imagine, predicting buck travel is tough — in fact, even more so than elsewhere because primary food sources tend to be more numerous in wilderness areas than in other habitat types. One good tactic is to set up an ambush close to these food sources where as many does as possible can be seen. During the breeding period, most of the larger wilderness bucks will be with does 90 percent of the time, perhaps even more. So, regardless of your preferred hunting style, concentrate your hunting hours near these family units now.

During the post-season period, bucks everywhere tend to be difficult to hunt. As a rule, we could expect our buck to return to his core area during this time. Hunting near his bedding area is a good bet, or we might try ambushes on patterns incorporating primary food sources in or near his core area.

When a mature wilderness buck is under heavy hunting pressure, he's an elusive animal. With so much cover to choose from, locating his sanctuary cover is usually difficult. Occasional rubs, droppings and tracks often are our best clues, but any disturbance could send him elsewhere. And, that "elsewhere" is a mighty big, confusing place in which to find him again.

Deer drives can work in wilderness habitat, but escape routes often are so numerous that it's difficult, if not impossible, to cover them all. One and two-man silent drives in small patches of cover occasionally can be productive if you understand the lay of the land and know where escape routes lead. But, you often have only the briefest of shot opportunities at big woods bucks on the move due to the overall amount of cover.

Hunting wilderness habitat certainly can be rewarding. In addition to whitetails, a variety of other wildlife species often are seen and a certain serenity usually is felt. It's just great to be in the woods. The difficulty of hunting the big woods usually means they hold some of those gray-faced monarchs seldom seen by humans. These are "wild" bucks in every way, and bagging one is an experience you'll always remember.

Chapter 18

Patterning
Fringe Bucks

Fringe habitat is a combination of open areas — agricultural fields, meadows, open hillsides or even beaver-cut clearings — and substantial blocks of cover. To qualify for this category, the cover must be large enough that deer seldom feel forced to leave it, even under heavy hunting pressure. This distinguishes it from woodlot habitat since bucks there can be forced to relocate their bedding grounds to different blocks of cover under moderate to heavy pressure.

Depending somewhat on the time of year, a fringe buck's primary food sources usually will be located along the periphery of the cover. This food source does not necessarily have to be touching the big woods, but it does have to be within a reasonable distance. The pattern, then, is one of moving from the heavy cover to a feeding area on or near its edge.

Actually, fringe habitat lies somewhere between woodlot and wilderness habitat types since it has characteristics of each. The cover is almost like that in a wilderness habitat; therefore, pressure simply causes a buck to move to another bedding area in the same block but seldom forces him to leave. Yet, fringe habitat is also like woodlot habitat in that agriculture or other open food sources are adjacent to or near the cover. The buck's food sources aren't located at random, like they often appear to be in wilderness habitat, but are along the fringe, where they're far easier to identify and locate.

Fringe habitat is common in nearly every U.S. state and Canadian province in which whitetails are hunted. It can be seen in

Saskatchewan's northern fringe, where agriculture meets the vast provincial forest, was where the author caught up with this massive, palmated non-typical. Photo by Marlin Parasiuk.

basic farm country, semi-wilderness and nearly everywhere else, except in traditional wilderness and prairie regions. Some of the classic prairie states, such as the Dakotas, Wyoming, Colorado (eastern), Nebraska, Montana (eastern) and others, have very few huge blocks of cover that would qualify for inclusion in this category. Fringe habitat can be found in remote areas or near substantial human populations.

Examples of fringe habitat might include an alfalfa field tucked against the border of unbroken provincial forest in Manitoba or an apple orchard adjacent to a big tract of timberland in Virginia. Of course, the amount and shape of the cover vary from one fringe habitat to the next, as does the percentage of cover present. Again, the common denominator is that the cover is large enough that the deer are not forced to seek other blocks of cover for bedding during daylight hours. Given this, we usually can predict where a buck is feeding and which chunk of cover he's using for bedding.

General patterns

Each habitat type has its tradeoffs that make bucks easier or more difficult to hunt. Prairie bucks are quite visible when they're on their feet, but it's difficult to predict their bedding locations, especially under high hunting pressure. Woodlot bucks frequently are seen in or near their multiple feeding areas, but it's difficult to identify which woodlot they're bedding in and which field they might travel to on a given day. Wilderness bucks often move freely during the day; however, it's more difficult to locate their bedding and feeding locations because these spots are so numerous and the cover can look rather homogenous. In fringe habitat, we might find that it's relatively easy to know where a buck is feeding and in which block of cover he's bedding but that it's difficult to know exactly where he's living within that cover. Regardless of the habitat, bucks quickly learn how to use the lay of the land to their advantage, particularly when they're feeling the heat from hunters.

Generally speaking, fringe habitats are characterized by the fact that the family units live along the fringe, or at least closer to it than do the bucks. So, when buck destinations center around does, the buck's general movement trend is toward the edge. Certainly, his rut-related activities are likely to be greatest at the edge or wherever the doe concentrations are located.

Outside the rut, the movement trend toward the fringe is also frequently seen when winter weather and its corresponding food scarcity bring bucks to the edge strictly for wintering/food reasons. In western Canada, for example, it's a recognized fact that many huge bucks show up at or after the end of season (December 1) along the fringes. They were not living there during the hunting season, and no one can be sure how far these bucks have traveled from the deep woods.

Patterns during the four periods

As before, let's follow our mature buck as he moves through fringe habitat so we can get a clear picture of why and how his travel patterns evolve. Once again, we'll do this through all four periods of

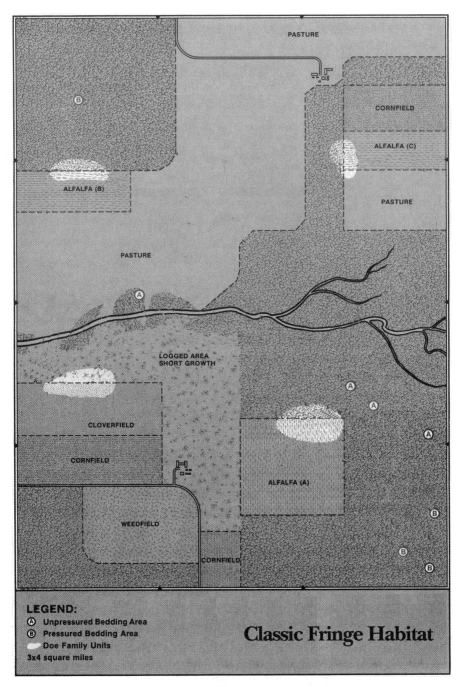

LEGEND:
(A) Unpressured Bedding Area
(B) Pressured Bedding Area
    Doe Family Units
3x4 square miles

Classic Fringe Habitat

the rut, under both lightly and heavily hunted conditions.

In the rut-preparation period without heavy pressure from hunters, we'd probably find the buck using a typical bedding site in the largest tract of cover in the area. Most really big fringe bucks I've

In fringe habitat, bucks seek security in a big woods setting but usually feed on nearby agriculture. This is a common habitat type throughout the whitetail's range. Photo by Bill Marchel.

located and hunted have been using larger blocks of cover as their core areas, so that's where I'll usually begin my scouting. In this case, our buck likely will have chosen a bedding site that's convenient to his primary food source but still is surrounded by a lot of woods. Just how close to the food source he'll bed now depends upon the amount of pressure — the heavier the pressure, the deeper in the woods he'll bed.

As in other habitats, our buck follows a relatively short pattern during the rut-preparation period. This is a time when food is the priority. The buck's pace of travel between bedding and feeding areas usually will be slow. Even as he travels, he frequently nibbles on the sap-filled browse of fall and spends considerable time rubbing trees along the way, especially after leaving his bed in late afternoon. Interestingly, this seems to be the case no matter how far the buck is moving to feed every evening. Rather than relocate his bedding site to a location much closer to his preferred feeding area, he simply travels farther each way, and he does so at a leisurely pace. In Saskatchewan one October, I hunted a fringe buck that was traveling more than two miles each day to reach a newly cut barley field, passing other less desirable fields along the way.

During the pre-breeding period, our buck has moved closer to the family unit in his core area and to his favorite line of scrapes. By now, his priority has shifted from food to females, and his range of travel has expanded dramatically. Normally, he first checks those scrapes in the family unit range nearest his core area, then moves on to others as he monitors the reproductive status of a large number of females. In most cases, his routes will follow connected cover where possible, but at other times, he might choose to take a more direct route and disregard security. This is the time of season when a hunter might see the buck crossing a field after sunrise and think, "He's leaving the feeding area late this morning." When in reality, the buck actually is running late in completing his nightly circuit of checking on does.

When the breeding period finally arrives, we might catch our buck doing something he'd almost never do during other periods of the hunting season — bed in a small island of cover far from the security of the big woods. And, he does it for only one reason — a hot doe. This is a pattern I've seen in nearly every region I've hunted.

For several years, I hunted along the North Saskatchewan River in northern Alberta. All along the river, the terrain was rough and choked with heavy brush since the river was far below the flatter, "tabletop" farmland above. During most of the year, the big bucks in this area stayed in and along the edge of this vast tract of heavy cover. But once the breeding period began, these bucks often could be seen with does several miles from the river, in flat farm country more like woodlot habitat. Once they were spooked, however, they'd head cross-country for the river.

When we'd make a deer drive through a small patch of bush out in the farm country, the buck would jump up and head across a wide-open field, which seemed at the time an unlikely escape route. When he'd hit the next patch of cover, even if it was fairly large, he'd go right through it and wouldn't stop until he reached the river bottom. Once we learned the pattern, we'd quickly head to the river to cut him off since we knew that's where he'd eventually end up even if he had been jumped five miles away.

During the post-breeding period, the breeding urge loosens its grip. Our buck has moved to a bedding site deeper in the woods but still in the core area he prefers. His range size is now larger than during the rut-preparation period, as he makes his last rounds looking for a late hot doe, but smaller than during the pre-breeding period. Of course, the buck:doe ratio has a great deal to do with his range size now, as increased competition for does will result in a larger travel pattern.

Our fringe buck's travel route actually varies little as hunting pressure increases, except that progressively more of his desired circuit will be covered during nighttime hours. But, the bedding locations are almost always different in heavy pressure situations. In the case of fringe habitat, the buck usually relocates his bedding site to another part of the same woods rather than vacating the cover block entirely. The new bedding area might be a place choked with heavy cedar and briar thickets, into which an undetected approach by a hunter would be nearly impossible. If hunting pressure becomes too heavy there, he'll simply move to yet another bedding location in the same woods.

During the breeding period, our pressured buck will be found in wherever his doe is. When too much pressure is applied to her preferred bedding site, she'll head for another known security area in her home range, with the big buck following.

Hunting tactics

Fringe habitat is one of my favorites because primary food sources, and thus the doe groups, usually are relatively easy to locate and most of the hunting is done deep in the woods. To know where the buck is feeding and where the does are located is to have half of the travel riddle solved and greatly enhances the chances for overall success. Normally, in fringe habitat, we at least know the most likely travel direction or block of cover where he's bedding, either of which is a big help. It's always easier to hunt a buck along a line between two points, even if one point is not exact, than it is to hunt along many lines radiating out from a central point.

Regardless of the rut period, I always begin scouting at the food sources because some type of buck sign will be present there. During the rut-preparation period, rubs will be present along the wood line where feeding is occurring. Rubs and scrapes should be

When bedding inside big blocks of cover, bucks often select a spot on the down-wind side of a thicket where they have good visibility into a more open area. By doing so, they can smell danger approaching from the thick upwind side and see danger coming from the more open downwind view. Photo by Neal Mishler.

visible during the pre-breeding period, numerous running tracks during the breeding period (bucks chasing does), and light rub and scrape activity during the post-breeding period. Large tracks are helpful for pinpointing buck locations anytime.

Outside the breeding period, one of my favorite tactics is a deep woods ambush. I generally prefer to use a treestand if possible. Tracks, trails, rubs and/or scrape lines leading to or from the feeding area would define the routes being used. Whether the stand should be placed closer to the field or the bedding site will depend on hunting pressure — the heavier the pressure, the closer to his bed we must position ourselves in order to see him in legal shooting light. Also, the more involved the buck is in pursuing does, the better our chances of finding him closer to the does and to the fringe. And finally, it makes a difference whether we're hunting in the morning or the evening, as morning stands usually need to be closer to bedding areas than do evening stands.

Fringe habitat usually offers enough security cover to allow a fair number of bucks to reach older ages even if pressure is substantial. Because of this and the agriculture so often nearby, fringe habitat is often associated with big bucks like this one. Photo by Troy Huffman.

When pressure on our buck is relatively high, he can be an especially tough nut to crack, particularly outside the breeding period. He's apt to change bedding locations from day to day if spooked, and he might become completely nocturnal. Without knowing exactly when he's leaving his bed in the evening, we're forced to set up an ambush as close to the bedding area as possible without getting so close that our presence is detected. Of course, knowing exactly where he's bedding is a difficult trick. I prefer to keep a safe distance until I can see what's happening, then gradually move closer or utilize a rut period change to get him in a different pattern.

Our fringe buck is also difficult to target during the breeding period, regardless of hunting pressure. His movements will be unpredictable during this time, and the only reasonable approach is to hunt family units or doe patterns and hope that you happen to be hunting the same one he's checking for a hot doe.

Without knowing exactly where the buck is bedded at any given time in fringe habitat, I generally hunt the trails with the most large tracks, rubs, scrapes or whatever other sign is most applicable at that time. To minimize the chance of him relocating to another food source without my realizing it, I also spot-check other feeding areas in the neighborhood to see if his fresh sign turned up there. A big buck adapts quickly to the presence of a hunter, and we must recognize when we or other persons have forced him into a reactionary pattern.

While scouting is always important, I believe it is of less importance in fringe country than your hunting technique. Here, hunting a big buck is much like a chess game: When one player makes a move, the other ponders it and moves accordingly. When we set up and hunt stands, scout, walk into or out of the woods, etc., we're making moves. The buck then makes his move by switching to another bedding area, utilizing a different travel pattern or food source or, if too much pressure is put on him, turning completely nocturnal.

What's the simple answer to killing such a deer? Sorry, there isn't one. Success in hunting mature bucks in fringe habitat comes from making the right moves, reacting wisely to his moves and playing the game out fully. It can be a tough game to win because we're on his home turf. But, the more we know about what the buck wants to do and why, the better our chances.

Chapter 19

Coping With Elevation Changes

F EW WHITETAIL BUCKS IN ANY PART OF NORTH AMERICA have a home
range that's completely flat. Most habitats have enough rise and
fall to the landscape to affect deer travel patterns, though some of
these features are far more dramatic than others. Elevation changes
don't represent a fifth category of habitat, as they exist in all four of
the types previously discussed. However, because they do play a
major role in determining bucks travel patterns, we won't have examined habitats in full until we've considered the effect topography has
on whitetails.

Elevation changes come in many shapes and forms. The most
obvious are large mountain ranges, such as the Rockies and
Appalachians, which always are characterized by a unique travel pattern. These two major ranges are quite different from each other,
since most Appalachian peaks have timber growing all the way to
their summits while many mountains in the Rockies top out above
timberline. But, mountains aren't the only places where elevation
changes affect whitetail patterns. Everywhere you look in deer country, there are high and low spots relative to the surroundings, such as
rolling hills, ravines, ridges, cliffs, knobs, valleys, creek bottoms,
gorges, etc.

In Alberta, Saskatchewan and Manitoba, for example, two predominant forms of elevation changes generally affect whitetail movement. One is the network of drainages that sprawl across the landscape. Especially in southern areas of these provinces, where most
brush and timber have been stripped away to increase agricultural
acreage, the wide, steep, brushy banks along drainages are the whitetail's primary bedding locations. Even where other cover exists, these
ravines provide a greater source of security cover than do other locations and thus are hangouts for many big bucks.

Rick Manos killed this 27-inch, record-class Montana buck by taking into account the influence of elevation. This buck was feeding low and bedding high. He killed him on a scrape line high near his bedding area. Photo by author.

The second type of elevation change in these provinces are low ridges, hills and knolls. The overall topography of central Canada seems rather flat, but most areas have some low ridges and hills affecting travel patterns to varying degrees, depending on the specific elevations, amounts and types of cover, etc.

Much of the Midwest has river and creek bottoms with hills rising above them. A significant amount of land along the Eastern Seaboard has foothills, ridges and rolling terrain, some of which is steep. Parts of Idaho, Montana, Wyoming, Colorado and Washington have a unique topography, with huge expanses of rolling farm country being cut by river breaks that steeply drop hundreds of feet to the rivers themselves. Instead of the normal river-bottom scenario, in which hills and ravines drop down to a flat and often farmed river bottom, this type of situation is just the opposite. The farmland is spread across a seemingly flat, "table-top" horizon, and gorges up to hundreds of feet deep drop to the rivers. In this scenario, deer bed low and climb upward to feed — a rather unusual occurrence in the world of whitetails.

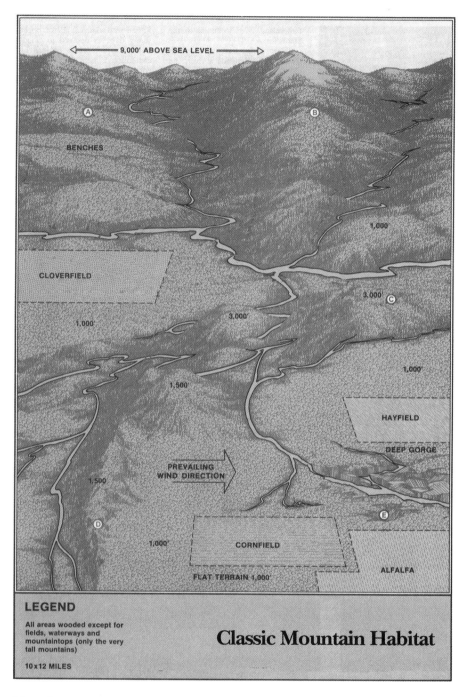

Travel patterns

Just as we can predict certain movement trends in the four habitat types, we also can count on deer to move in certain patterns

206

This photo shows a typical wind pattern in mountainous terrain. The wind generally follows the contours and is fairly consistent near the tops and more erratic in the valleys. Bucks prefer to bed high on sidehills, often on benches or points, where they can see some distance downwind below them and smell anything upwind above them. This scenario applies to most types of elevated habitat, whether knobs, cliffs, ridges, etc., so long as they are large. However, bucks often bed on the very tops of small knobs and hills. Photo by author.

with regard to elevation. These patterns will change depending on the geographic nature and degree of elevation, but they are predictable nonetheless.

To illustrate several types of movement, we'll be discussing patterns of deer relating to tall mountains, small mountains, foothills, low hills and ravines. I realize it's unlikely that you'd find all of these topographic forms where you hunt, but it's still interesting and helpful to look at their impact on whitetails.

Without again getting into the rut's affects on whitetail patterns, suffice it to say that all bucks expand their travel distances noticeably to include more family units, regardless of elevation or habitat type, as the breeding period nears. Also, in situations where bucks live most of the year high on mountainsides, there will be a trend toward bedding at lower elevations as the rut heats up, especially as the pre-breeding period comes to a close and the first does become receptive. Of course, this is merely the bucks' means of relocating closer to the action, as the drainages (lower elevations) contain most of the family units in an area and the buck must move down the mountain to reach them.

In the Rockies of Montana, Idaho or British Columbia, it isn't uncommon to encounter bucks bedding at around 6,000 feet above sea level during the rut-preparation period. Several years ago, I killed a buck at 7,000 feet in Montana. His sign was so plentiful in that location that there was little doubt he'd been living there. Also, while hunting elk in Montana at elevations of 6,000 to 8,000 feet in October, I've seen enough whitetail bucks and their sign to convince me that many bucks live in small, isolated pockets in the high country. Their travel distances are short in the rut-preparation period, just as elsewhere. But almost without exception, these bucks begin ranging to lower elevations sometime during the pre-breeding or breeding period, and they don't return to the high country during the winter, especially in locales where heavy snow accumulation is likely. Bucks there may even migrate in December or January if snow levels are substantial.

In many mountainous areas, especially those with agriculture in the valleys, some bucks will bed high and travel to the valley floor each night to feed. As the rut progresses, their bedding sites predictably become lower, until they begin living among the does just prior to the breeding period. Generally, does and younger bucks live at lower elevations all year, though this is not a hard-and-fast rule.

Where pressure on mountain bucks is substantial, the animals will do what they must to avoid being hassled. For instance, I've seen them bed in thickets on hillsides so steep that you almost had to hang onto trees to navigate. As a rule, we can say that if "mountain" bucks feel pressure from people, they will tend to move into higher and/or more rugged pockets for bedding. Most hunters in this type of terrain approach the deer from below.

Among the most unique and predictable travel pattern features in areas with significant elevation changes are the trail systems and bedding sites utilized. Generally, the "vertical" trails denote travel to/from bedding and feeding areas, while the "horizontal" trails normally are found within bedding or feeding/rut areas. Where there's

This buck is standing in a typical preferred bedding site in terrain with elevation extremes. Bucks like steep hillsides with small benches where they can lay on the edge to watch their descending downwind side. Photo by Roman Jaskolski.

no agriculture present in the valley floor or other low elevation areas, horizontal trails along creeks and rivers are especially common. Vertical trails generally branch off such feeding routes and climb straight up (actually, more often, angle up) the mountainside. Some vertical trails might follow a tributary stream vertically if deer feed along its edge as they move up to bed or down to feed. At some point, though, these trails will become horizontal and that's a sure clue that the bedding area has been entered.

Bedding sites

Bedding sites typically are predictable by the wind direction and type of elevation. When possible, deer prefer to bed high and travel to lower elevations to feed and carouse. If you're aware of this and can interpret sign as you go, you often can start to zero in on a buck's probable bedding site before you jump him. This bedding habit is so consistent that it plays a major role in my scouting and predicting of travel patterns.

The buck that beds high has two major advantages. The first is

In the hilly country pictured here, as in more mountainous terrain, bedding usually will occur near the upper one-third of the hills, feeding is at or toward the bottom, vertical trails connect the bedding and feeding areas and horizontal trails appear near the bedding zone. Photo by author.

his obvious wind advantage because of the way thermals move up and down mountains and the manner in which wind currents pass over mountain crests. Thermal air currents rise and fall along the faces of mountains and hills in response to changing air temperatures. When temperatures are warmer, which is the case during most of the daylight hours, the air is rising. For a buck bedded high, this means his afternoon descent from the mountain will put the wind in his face. That's a clear advantage for any prey species that depends heavily on its nose for detecting danger.

After sunset, when the temperature falls, the cooling air becomes heavier and moves down the mountain. Again, the buck has the advantage in early morning as he climbs back up the hill into the wind, reaching his bedding site before the air warms much and the thermals shift directions. In most of the areas I've hunted, the morning thermal shift occurs between 8:30 and 9:30 a.m., depending on the weather. It's no coincidence that this is also about the same time most mountain bucks bed.

Besides the thermals, bucks, and deer in general, choose bedding sites on the prevailing downwind side of knobs and ridgetops. Occasionally, they will bed on the top itself, but more often, they'll choose a spot just below the rim where they can look down on what they can't smell. All the while, they'll be smelling what they can't see as the wind passes over the top and comes down to them on the back edge. For anyone hunting such bucks, a lesson in the difficulty of approaching bedded deer will soon be learned.

The second advantage for bucks that bed high is the abundance of ideal escape routes available to them. Again, when possible, bucks prefer to bed on ground that rises in the middle and drops off on the sides, rather than in bowl-shaped hollows. When he's bedded high, not only can a buck spot danger much more quickly, he also has an escape route off the opposite rim that will immediately put him out of sight of his pursuer, no matter which direction danger might approach. On the other hand, should he bed in a valley bottom, he's likely to be visible from either side as he escapes. Thus, you'll seldom find bucks bedded at the bottom of depressions in which they can be trapped.

Depending somewhat on hunting pressure and the period of the rut, mature bucks are apt to bed in a zone in the upper one-third of smaller mountains and ridges. In extremely high mountains, they may bed somewhat lower. Although many hunters might not want to believe it, bucks think nothing of descending 2,000 to 3,000 feet to feed each night in the valley floor.

Mountain bedding sites usually are located on one of two types of terrain features — benches or knobs. Bucks often bed on small benches, in many cases less than 20 yards wide, and they'll even look for a small knob that protrudes out farther than the lip for an added visual advantage. A buck so bedding depends more on sighting approaching danger than on smelling it. Another likely bedding spot is on a spine or ridge that traverses the mountain's face. In this type of scenario, the buck usually will choose to lie below the ridgetop on the downwind side, thus allowing the buck to depend equally on his senses of smell and vision for security.

Another type of bedding spot popular with bucks is one very near the top of a peak or ridge. In most cases, a trail will follow along or near the top itself, on which the buck will travel before dropping off either side to bed, depending on the wind direction. Both horizonal and vertical trails will be present in this pattern.

Completing the picture

While many of the examples I've provided thus far have been from true mountain regions, much more subtle land forms also can have major impacts on buck patterns, especially in regard to choice of bedding sites. Regardless of how big or small a "mountain" might be, bucks will use it in trying to get an edge on predators. Look for bedding sites on the downwind side of the top of various land forms, where bucks can enjoy advantages in seeing, smelling and escaping from danger. Often, when knobs and ridges are not much higher than the surrounding area, bucks actually will lie on the ridgetops themselves. They prefer to bed on rises even a few feet above the surrounding area when that's the only choice they have because this gives them a slight edge when looking for predators. Although not as dramatic, horizonal and vertical trails still will be present with even minimal elevation changes.

Finally, some bucks will choose to live in yet another type of elevation environment, one we might even call "negative" elevation. In such situations, the buck actually lives below his feeding area and climbs higher to feed. As noted earlier, this pattern is far more common in some regions than in others. As a rule, deer in these scenarios prefer to bed nearer the top of the ravine than the bottom — usually in the upper one-third of the cover. Again, trails will descend from the fields somewhat vertically and become horizonal when they reach preferred bedding sites. Depending on the type of browse and cover along the creek bottom, trails might or might not be present there. The deer have little reason to go to the waterway itself on a regular basis unless some type of desired browse is present.

Hopefully, this and the previous four chapters have given you a new way of looking at whitetail habitats and the ways in which they are used by bucks during hunting season. Obviously, each situation is unique; however, the principles we've discussed here are universal. It's just a matter of studying a location from a logical perspective and with an eye for detail, then applying accumulated knowledge to put yourself one step ahead of the buck you're after. It can be a lot of work, but it's the kind of labor we all love. We call it hunting!

APPLIED HUNTING TACTICS

Chapter 20

Translating Patterns Into Hunting Tactics

THE WHITETAILS WE HUNT TODAY may be the same species hunted by our forefathers, but they are not the same animal. The modern buck has evolved and adapted to his environment. Decades of survival in a world of traffic, house dogs, subdivisions, decoys, grunt calls, scents, treestands, long-range rifles and proficient hunters have created a different animal. Bucks hunted primarily from treestands have learned to look up, those hunted from roads have mastered how to avoid vehicles and bucks pursued by hounds have figured out how to throw the pack off the trail.

Whitetail deer, more than any other big game animal in the world, possess a unique ability to adapt, whether it be to different or changing habitats or to new pressures, human and otherwise. Today's bucks tend to be more nocturnal and streetwise to human movement and behavior. They are the masters of evasion and the ultimate survivor in the world of big game!

Since the game we hunt is adapting so rapidly to all we're throwing at him, we hunters also must adapt new tactics and strategies if we're to be successful in our pursuit of these animals. Simply putting up a stand and sitting it out for the season isn't enough. We must be flexible and innovative, developing new strategies and tactics and mixing them up to keep the buck from patterning us. We must avoid thinking and acting like the predictable masses.

As we've said, all bucks are on some type of travel pattern. More than ever, we must unravel as much of that pattern as possible in hopes of finding vulnerable points. Hunting individual big bucks

After figuring out a buck's travel pattern, you still have to kill him. That's where hunting skill and sound tactics come into play. No, that's not a mounted buck ... but if the hunter was paying attention, he soon would be. Photo by Roman Jaskolski.

can at times be frustrating and requires a different mind set from that of simply hunting a general area, but by concentrating on a particular big buck and being creative in our approach, the payoff can be big — literally. The decisions concerning where to hunt, which tactic to use and when to be there should be determined according to the buck's travel pattern, period of the rut and many other relevant factors; not arbitrarily.

As one becomes more familiar with a particular buck's travel pattern and range, it should soon become apparent that several ambush locations and tactics have the potential of working. Hopefully, it will also become clear that the combination of productive locations and tactics changes throughout the season. There is never only one tactic or one place to kill a certain buck, but there are definitely choices that offer the best odds of success. As this book has emphasized, a complete hunter must be able to unravel travel patterns and pick a likely spot, but he must also be versatile and pro-

To maximize the odds of success for big whitetails, you need to find a specific buck to hunt, figure out what he's doing then lay out a strategy. That's exactly what the author and well-known Texas biologist Bob Zaiglin did when they teamed up to rattle in this 25-inch 10-pointer for the author after seeing him earlier in the hunt. Photo by David Morris.

ficient in all the necessary tactics; not just a specialist in any one or two tactics.

Most hunters hunt a certain way or choose specific tactics out of habit. Perhaps it's the standard for the area or what was learned from a hunting mentor. Their particular hunting approach may work to a degree, but quite often, another tactic exists that is better. In many cases, the most popular local tactic is the least effective since the big bucks have figured out how to avoid that particular type of pressure.

Many factors affect our choice of tactics, and some of them change throughout the season. Geography or terrain type play heavily into our choices. For example, in wilderness regions, deer tend to move throughout the day and there are no roads, fields, fencelines and such to direct travel or hunting pressure. Our choice of tactics there will certainly be different from that of woodlots surrounded by agriculture, where the bucks are sure to be familiar with humans and nearly nocturnal. Laws, season dates, weather, cover types and hunting pressure are just a few of the other influences affecting our choice of tactics.

Where and when a buck travels are primary elements of a travel pattern. The where side of the equation can more easily be unravelled because the buck leaves sign wherever he travels and spends time. With knowledge of his pattern, we can then make common sense choices for ambush locations and other strategies.

"When" a buck moves can be tougher to figure out than where and often requires an educated guess. While where a buck travels certainly has some impact on our choice of tactics, it is when he moves that has the most influence. A totally nocturnal buck requires a different strategy from one that frequently moves during daylight hours. In the following discussion of the various tactics, it's important to keep in mind that when and how much a buck moves in the daytime greatly affects our choice of tactics.

I would also point out that an in-depth discussion of hunting strategy and various tactics is another book in itself. Here, we will attempt to examine each tactic in an overview perspective with emphasis on their relationship to the four periods of the rut and buck movement.

Chapter 21

Tactics For When The Buck Comes To You

T HERE ARE BASICALLY TWO CATEGORIES OF HUNTING TACTICS — one is where the buck comes to us and the second is when we go to him. This chapter covers the first category — where ambush is used and the buck comes to us.

Stand and ambush hunting

The various forms of ambush, which include treestand hunting, ground blinds, baiting, rattling and calling, are the most universal and popular tactics in the country. This group also happens to include my favorites, although the group does have one major shortfall — an ineffectiveness on nocturnal bucks. Still, the tactics within this grouping work extremely well when used properly.

Let's begin with treestands and their associated equipment. Needless to say, there is a vast array of types and brands of treestands and related paraphernalia. Portables are the most popular and can be set up quickly and quietly with the aid of screw-in or strap-on steps, portable ladders, tree-climbing spikes, etc. Depending upon the manufacturer and particular style, they are relatively light, portable, inexpensive and can be hidden from other hunters. They are generally my favorite type of stand.

Portables need to be relatively small if they are to be carried long distances or transported through thick cover. The very smallest stands, however, can be uncomfortable if long-term sitting is required. When sitting a half-day or longer at a time, I often use larger styles of portables for added comfort, especially if I think I may

Ambush hunting, which means treestand hunting to most hunters, is the most popular method across the country and certainly one of the most productive. Photo by Bill Marchel.

use it for several sittings.

Self-climbers are often larger, noisier to erect and more difficult to transport long distances through heavy cover than the lock-on type portables, but they tend to go up faster and are often more comfortable once erected. If I have a stand site I plan to hunt for several days, I generally "self-climb" the stand up the tree the first time, anchor it in place then access the stand via screw-in steps thereafter. This way, I get the best of both worlds — comfort and quiet. Many areas don't have the straight, limbless trees suitable for a self-climber, making portables with screw-in steps more versatile.

A permanent stand can be a portable left in the same spot for years (or all season), or it may be permanently built in a tree or on the ground. The main difference between portable and permanent stands is that, regardless of their architecture, permanents tend to be hunted repeatedly, to the point, in fact, that local deer soon become aware of their presence and may eventually learn to avoid them,

Taking big bucks consistently is no accident. It's the result of hard work, planning and effective tactics. Dwight Green of Iowa proves that ambush hunting where big bucks live can produce fantastic results. The wide buck on the left scores 187 2/8 and has an inside spread of 30 3/8 inches, the widest of any buck in the record book. Photo by author.

especially the bigger bucks. With frequently hunted permanent stands, the deer invariably look directly at the stand before looking elsewhere. It doesn't take many hunters traipsing to and hunting the same stand, usually spooking deer each time, before deer are tuned in to the danger.

Bow stands generally should be set lower than those intended for gun hunting. The reason is that bowhunters need the better angle on the deer's body and the larger target area presented from the lower elevation. Depending upon the particular tree, the terrain, the canopy and the overall situation, I tend to place gun stands 15 to 25 feet high and bow stands 10 to 20 feet above the ground. If the deer are clued in to treestands, I may hunt higher. In areas like Montana or Canada where most deer have never seen a hunter in a treestand, I frequently hunt lower.

All treestand sitters should have their silhouette broken by limbs, brush and trees. I don't care for camouflage fabric around treestands. It tends to be too conspicuous and flaps in the wind, occasionally making noise or attracting the deer's attention.

Noise is a major consideration when s t a n d - h u n t i n g . Nothing aggravates me more than a stand that squeaks every time I move. Quiet clothing is also important, especially in cold country where noise carries farther and hunters tend to wear more clothing. Also, a silent approach is important. Obviously, it's critical not to walk across the path where an approaching buck may pass.

Any responsible treestand discussion must include the issue of safety. I am amazed each year at the large number of accidents I

Ground blinds, even as simple as sitting next to a stump or leaning against a tree, are very effective and offer the advantage of convenience, silence and flexibility. Rattling, as this hunter is doing, is another tactic that depends on the buck coming to the hunter. Photo by Bill Marchel.

hear about just during my conversations with other hunters. I can only assume that the overall number is staggering. Most accidents can be blamed on carelessness, slips, falling asleep and other hunter errors and is seldom because of equipment failure. Treestand manufacturers, especially those established for several years, have well-tested products. Many accidents occur while the hunter is climbing up or down the tree or when getting into the stand. While actually

During his earlier outfitting days, the author rattled in this high 160s 15-pointer in South Texas for Jerry Ippileto. Photo by author.

climbing, I recommend the use of a harness or rope-type belt that goes around the upper body and also loops around the tree, allowing the hunter's hands to be free while climbing. This is the same concept pole-climbers used before power buckets. Safety belts should also be used while in the stand.

Ground stands can be very effective in many instances and share obvious similarities with treestands. The decided advantage elevated stands have over ground blinds is that the hunter can see better and that scent is less of a problem. On the other hand, ground blinds have the advantage of being quick, quiet, safe and simple. I often simply sit on a stump or rest against a tree, especially at first light when trying to catch bucks on their way back to their bedding area. In such set-ups, I'm usually hunting close to bedding areas and cannot go in the previous day to set up a stand. Many times, even if a stand is set up, the wind may change and that stand can't be hunted. By using a ground blind, I can easily move to a place where the wind is more favorable.

Many hunt their stands regardless of the wind direction. This is a big mistake when hunting an individual buck. The first time he passes downwind and smells the hunter, the effectiveness of that stand for that buck has been diminished. I try not to hunt any stand unless the wind is blowing in the opposite direction or at least at a 90 degree angle to where I expect the buck to come from.

Successful stand or ambush tactics require some degree of buck movement. This activity may be natural, meaning the buck moves of his own accord, or other hunters may initiate movement. Stand and ambush hunting tactics are tied to deer movement patterns more than any other tactics.

During the rut-preparation period, overall daytime buck movement is relatively low, with most taking place early and late in the day. However, because the deer are cautious now, the cover is thick and the buck patterns are somewhat predictable, stand-hunting is the best game in town, especially for bowhunting. Generally, stand placement should be closer to the bedding area than to the food source. During the pre-breeding period, activity increases and the effectiveness of ambush tactics is enhanced. As the period progresses, the stand site should be moved ever closer to the high-interaction areas and doe groups.

The breeding period has the highest daytime buck activity, but stand placement can be difficult because bucks are now covering such a vast range. A site that allows the hunter to look over as many does as possible is often the most productive. During the post-breeding period, bucks are more nocturnal, requiring stand placement to again be nearer the bedding site.

Rattling and calling

Rattling and calling are also tactics where the deer comes to us. In the last decade, deer calling has been in vogue and a great deal has been written about it, not to mention the many videos and seminars presented on the subject. Put into proper perspective, rattling and calling are simply additional tactics that can be incorporated into other methods. They can be very useful at particular times of the season and in certain places, but their success varies widely in different parts of North America.

Rattling is one of the older forms of deer calling. It simulates the sounds of bucks engaged in a deadly battle over the right to breed a hot doe. When these battles occur, a receptive doe is almost always on the scene. Other bucks suspect that may be the case and come looking for the doe. The grunt call works for much the same reason as rattling — bucks often grunt in the presence of hot does, thus other bucks come in search of the does. Numerous audio and video tapes are available demonstrating calling and rattling techniques. In reality, the actual sounds created are only a part of the success formula.

Timing is one of the most critical elements of effective calling. There is a relatively narrow window of prime time. Rattling and calling are both tied to rutting activity. In the rut-preparation period, the bucks are not yet interested enough in breeding to respond. Later, once the actual breeding period begins, the bigger, more dominant bucks are with receptive does most of the time and are not as likely to respond. The prime window is the two to three-week pre-breeding period just prior to the first does coming into estrus, with the last of those days being the absolute best time for either form of calling. Response during the post-breeding is generally low unless buck competition is extremely high.

Vital factors in any calling method are an undetected approach and a proper set-up. If a buck is tipped off to the hunter's presence, it's a near-certainty he won't respond. Knowledge of bedding areas or where you think the buck will come from is necessary to get within a buck's hearing distance without disturbing him.

A proper set-up requires a favorable wind direction and adequate visibility. Nearly all bucks will respond on the downwind side. The hunter must set up where he can see downwind as far as he thinks a buck can smell him, which means at least 50 to 200 yards, depending on conditions. As much cover as possible should also be adjacent to the downwind area so he'll feel comfortable when approaching. Bucks are usually reluctant to cross open terrain.

Many factors influence the overall success of rattling and calling, paramount being the competition among bucks. When does far outnumber bucks, competition is low. The result is fewer rubs and

After four days in a frigid treestand in Saskatchewan, David Morris shot this 350-pound 10-pointer as he worked a scrape line. Photo by Carl Frohaug.

scrapes, less buck travel and lower response to rattling and calling. Extreme hunting pressure, free-ranging dogs and other disturbances also tend to reduce response.

Baiting

Baiting deer is a somewhat controversial tactic that is legal in some states and not in others. Many argue that a pile of corn, apples or grain is no different than a cornfield, an apple orchard or a grain-field. Others contend it takes unfair advantage of the deer and is too effective. The intent here is not to debate the merits of baiting but to briefly discuss the tactic.

Baiting is nothing more than a glorified food source and will be most attractive when the weather is extreme and/or where food is otherwise scarce or of low quality. Consequently, response to baiting will be slowest during the rut-preparation period and higher in the pre-breeding and breeding periods. Interestingly, in the post-breeding period, the attractiveness of baiting is only moderate to start with because the deer, especially the older bucks, are so worn from the rut, but the appeal of baiting increases as the period progresses. Overall, deer in cold climates must feed more — and thus take to bait better — than those in milder climates.

While mature bucks certainly will feed on baits, the bulk of the feeding is actually done by does (and young bucks), at least during daylight hours. As breeding nears, mature bucks begin visiting these doe concentrations heavily, just as they would any doe concentration. During the pre-breeding and breeding periods particularly, good bucks are frequently killed near baits, but more because the does are there than because of the food.

Think of baits as fields with a desirable food source. That's basically how the deer, particularly mature bucks, treat them. During hunting season, big bucks are seldom seen in open fields during daylight hours, but at night, they feed and search for hot does there. Baits are visited in much the same way, except that baits in heavy cover are frequented more during the daytime because of their protection and isolation. Like the fields, the better big buck hunting often is on the trails leading to and from the bait and around the scrape lines so often found near the baits, and not over the baits themselves.

Decoys

The widespread use of decoys is relatively new in deer hunting and has some application. Although doe and buck decoys are available, buck decoys seem more useful. This, of course, depends on the region and the level of buck competition.

The biggest advantage I see in decoying is for the bowhunter. The decoy can be used to help lure the buck within bow range and to distract the buck while the archer draws and shoots. On the negative side, stationary decoys are harder for deer to see than one would imagine. Bucks often walk pass a decoy and never recognize it. Safety is also a consideration. They should be marked with some blaze orange. Essentially, decoying is a short-range tactic that still requires the hunter to make a good stand-site selection based on prevailing travel patterns. Once the buck has come onto the scene, then a decoy may prove helpful.

Mock scrapes and rubs

Creating artificial scrapes and rubs can have some effect on buck movement but is not likely to move bucks any significant distance. I don't think bucks can be made to regularly check scrapes or visit rubs (artificial ones or those made by other bucks) much outside their normal travel pattern. After all, most of their routine is dictated by the presence and patterns of does. If the goal is to move a buck a couple of hundred yards or so, as the case may be when hunting near a property line or when bowhunting, the possibility of success exists. The use of a doe-in-heat scent and/or a buck's tarsal gland hung in a tree may help to be more convincing.

Mock scrapes and rubs are most likely to be effective during the pre-breeding period. Most big bucks are not routinely checking rubs and scrapes during the breeding period, and rut activity is too low during rut-preparation and post-breeding periods for mock rubs and scrapes to appeal much to bucks.

Chapter 22

Tactics For When You Go To The Buck

THERE ARE MANY SITUATIONS WHERE HUNTERS MOVE to the buck or take a more offensive approach. Let's now look at some of those tactics.

Still-hunting

Still-hunting, slip-hunting, stop-and-go and walking are all terms used to describe this popular hunting method. I enjoy this form of hunting more than any other, and it can be very productive under certain conditions. In other situations, there are better choices. Like every other tactic we've discussed, still-hunting is far more successful when there is substantial understanding of travel patterns in the area. Simply walking at random relies solely on luck.

I often still-hunt early in the process of hunting a certain buck to establish his location and scout out his travel pattern prior to focusing on a particular vulnerability in his pattern. True, I prefer to have most of my scouting done on a particular buck prior to the time of actual hunting. That's not always possible, and besides, periodic information updates are needed that can only be acquired on the ground. Still-hunting is a great way to hunt, scout and learn. I have killed several good bucks while doing this, but mostly after I had already begun to focus in on the buck.

Sometimes you have to go to the buck and try to make something happen. The author, with his brother's help, walked up this mid-160s 10-pointer in an eastern Montana river bottom. Photo by W.C. Idol.

When employing this still-hunting/scouting method, I pay attention to the usual factors. First, I check the wind to be sure it is favorable for my general travel direction. Where my route takes me and when I arrive there is planned according to what pattern I think the buck is on. Quite often, I'll reach certain points and sit or stand for a few minutes to perhaps as long as an hour or two. All the while, I'm gathering new information and reacting logically to what it tells me.

Let's look at an example of a day of still-hunting/scouting. Before light, I walk into an area to watch a crossing at the end of a strip of woods used by the deer to leave the fields and head into the big woods. I stay there until I feel all the bucks have cleared the fields. Next, I move into the big woods (bedding area) and do some rattling and calling. In the process, I discover an old fenceline and see a big buck chase a doe across it. Knowing a hot doe is in the area,

Two or three-man drives can be very productive. One of the good things about them is that the deer often move out slowly and cautiously, as this buck is doing, giving the hunter a chance for a sure shot. Photo by Ed Wolfe.

I sit there for a couple of hours to see what happens. I see a chase cross the fenceline a quarter-mile farther down. I move there and wait an hour. The weather turns hot and windy so I know most of the deer have laid down. I walk around until mid-afternoon, when I discover a hot scrape line along an old logging road running into the fenceline. I sit there until dark and decide that's where I'm going to hang my stand to hunt the buck I saw earlier.

In general, still-hunting requires that the deer be moving somewhat and that the cover lends itself to this method. If deer are bedded, they almost always move off without giving you a look or a shot. If the cover is too thick or the approach too noisy, they hear you long before you see them. The ideal set up is when deer are on the move, visibility is 100 yards or more and cutlines, old roadbeds or some type of travel lanes allow a quiet approach. As for when still-hunting works best relative to the four periods of the rut, the pre-breeding period is good and the breeding period is the best. The tactic is no better than a fair choice during the rut-preparation period and something less than that in the post-breeding.

Successful still-hunting requires more skill and experience than just about any other tactic. The hunter must be able to spot deer in the woods before they see him. That takes experience. Walking quietly, which is partly a natural talent and some acquired skill, is a requirement. Contrary to what many think, walking quietly requires much more effort than simply walking. Placing each footfall exactly right is strenuous effort. There's also the need to react quickly and shoot straight, something at which not all hunters are adept.

A brief mention of footwear and clothing for still-hunting is also in order. I generally wear a soft rubber-bottomed, leather-topped boot that is supple enough to feel sticks beneath my feet. Hard leather soles are the worst for quiet walking. Also, choose boots with bottom surfaces as small as possible to minimize contact with the ground. Quiet clothing is also essential. All the layers need to be soft and quiet, but the outer shell in particular must be quiet so that limbs and brush will not cause scraping noises.

Road hunting

I hesitate mentioning this tactic because road-hunting, even where legal, is often controversial. But, it is popular in many parts of North America — Canada, Texas, Mexico and areas of the West in particular. Many question the ethics of this tactic because abuses often occur, such as shooting from the highway, trespassing, chasing deer with the vehicle, etc. Again, the intent here is not a debate of ethics, but I would point out that local laws should be observed and respect given the landowners.

This concept relies on the exposure factor. Simply putting on miles in good deer country will result in some sightings and opportunities. More than any other form of hunting, deer must be on the move for road-hunting to be productive, making the pre-breeding and breeding periods the best time.

Make no mistake — successful road hunting is an art. The masters know an area very well and have a good idea of when and where the bucks move. They are aware of deer crossings, primary feeding fields, doe concentrations, seldom-used roads and fields where a buck might be intercepted. They will often park at vantage points overlooking such places at high movement periods. Surprisingly,

The author had found this buck earlier and tried in vain to wait him out. With time running out in the hunt, he finally had to go in after him. Sometimes, a hunter has to force the action. Photo by David Morris.

most deer are not spooked by stationary vehicles, especially along roads and in fields where they are accustomed to parked machinery, farm trucks, etc.

Probably the most specialized of all road-hunting is Texas "high-racking," which is perfectly legal in the Lone Star State. A platform, which basically amounts to a mobile stand, is mounted high above a vehicle. Then, the ranch roads are driven while the hunter watches from his elevated perch. While it sounds easy, bucks become educated to this tactic very quickly. Many ranches won't allow high-racking because too much of it will adversely affect deer movement. In reality, high-racks are probably more useful as stands that can be easily moved from place to place and set up than as road-hunting vehicles.

Deer drives

As I've mentioned before, many of today's big bucks are practically nocturnal during much of hunting season. Even those that move some during the day, do so very sparingly and usually in thick cover. For bucks that seldom expose themselves during the daytime, as is often the case during parts of the rut-preparation period and most of the post-breeding period, some type of forced movement tactic is essential. Deer drives are the foremost form of forced movement.

Traditional deer drives usually involve a line of several drivers, or pushers, proceeding through some piece of cover suspected of holding deer in an effort to move the deer to hunters posted at strategic escape routes at the other end. This is an age-old tactic for all types of big game, including whitetails. This traditional drive, however, is not my favorite type of drive, especially when I'm focused on hunting an individual buck.

First, big bucks generally prefer to bed in larger blocks of cover. Consequently, more standers and pushers are required for a successful drive. This means there are many exit possibilities, making it unlikely that you individually will be in the right place at the right time. You may have put in many days locating and patterning this particular buck only to have him pushed to another hunter. Also, this type of drive, if unsuccessful, may spook the buck so badly that he will move to another area and/or become more nocturnal. Of

It seems that many of the true giants are either found dead, shot under unusual circumstances or taken as a result of some type of forced movement. That was the case with the new world record typical. Milo Hanson of Biggar, Saskatchewan, claimed this now-famous 213 5/8-point typical on a deer drive. Photo by Gordon Whittington, courtesy WHITETAIL *magazine.*

course, there's always the problem of trying to judge and shoot a buck that in all likelihood will be running flat out.

I prefer, instead, a modified version of the traditional drive that has been very effective for me over the last few years. It involves only one or two pushers and one or two posted hunters. Most of the time when I employ this tactic, it's one pusher and one stander. For this to work, both hunters must be familiar with the terrain, otherwise you will spend most of the day looking for each other. It also requires some knowledge of our buck's travel patterns, particularly his bedding areas and escape routes. Where there is substantial hunting pressure, I often begin these type drives at mid-morning and continue until mid-afternoon. During this time, fewer hunters are in the woods and the bucks are generally bedded.

The key to this tactic is to push the buck only a relatively short distance (300 to 500 yards) and to set up to ambush him inside the cover as opposed to posting on the perimeter. It's difficult to push big bucks into the wide open spaces unless he has no other options, and it's equally difficult to keep bucks moving in one direction in front of pushers for any substantial distance.

Such a hunt would go something like this. Starting with a good idea of where I think the buck is and where he's likely to go when jumped, my pusher and I map our strategy. Then, we move into position, careful not to tip off the buck to our presence. I set up some 300 to 500 yards away from where I think the buck may be jumped at a point I think the buck may pass by. At a prearranged time, the pusher begins a silent zigzag drive toward me. His path must be unpredictable, silent and irregular so the buck can't figure out exactly which way he's traveling. If the buck can get a fix on the pusher's direction of travel, he will often circle behind him. The pusher should make just enough noise to be certain the buck is actually jumped but not enough to allow the buck to track him by a steady noise. Eventually, he will reach my position and the process is quietly repeated.

This tactic is far from foolproof. Bucks often go the wrong way, and standers and drivers sometimes get turned around. Positives for this type of drive are that bucks often slip slowly past the stander and/or frequently stop to look back toward the pusher, affording an opportunity to judge him and get a good shot. And, of course,

235

there's the simple exposure factor. Big bucks that have been spooked are subject to go anywhere and don't always conform to the "plan," but a nocturnal buck moving around in your immediate area offers you much greater odds of success than does a bedded buck.

Miscellaneous forced movement

Another unorthodox tactic I've successfully used on nocturnal bucks is to identify a bedding area, go to the area an hour or two before daylight (before the buck arrives) then set up a quiet portable stand in hopes of catching him just at daylight when he returns to bed. There's a downside, though. If the buck comes in and beds down but we don't get a shot, it's nearly impossible to get out of the stand without spooking him. I would use this tactic only as a last resort, not for early in a hunt.

Another productive tactic, although not as controllable as I would like, is to anticipate peak periods of hunting pressure, such as Saturdays or opening days, then set up along escape routes in hopes of ambushing bucks moved by other hunters. This tactic is generally best early on when hunting pressure first becomes heavy enough to move substantial numbers of deer that are still relatively undisturbed. It declines in effectiveness once deer have reacted to pressure.

Hopefully, it has become obvious that a strategy for hunting a specific buck must be flexible, adaptable and balanced with a liberal amount of common sense. All the influences on travel patterns, including the four periods of the rut, we've discussed so far are intended to prompt one's thinking as to cause and effect. If a particular weather condition suggests that the deer should be moving, a choice of tactics that capitalize on deer movement should be selected. If extreme hunting pressure dictates that the bucks will be nocturnal or bedded, then forced movement may be in order. As the pre-breeding period shifts to full-scale breeding, scrape hunting and rattling might be replaced by a stand in a high-interaction area where lots of deer can be seen. All of the cause-and-effect influences just described become especially effective when they are matched to what we've learned about travel patterns.

Of course, our overall strategy is not as simple as it appears on the surface. Almost always, there are several factors influencing our

Still-hunting can be very effective, but it takes the right kind of country, the right conditions and a skilled hunter to make the most of it. Photo by author.

choice of tactics, each with its own importance and many overriding others. A full-moon might indicate midday activity, but a pack of hounds may be running deer in the same area or a group of hunters might be putting on an organized deer drive at midday, either of which would cause us to alter a midday hunting plan. We must factor in all the elements, weigh their impact against each other then select the most logical strategy and tactic.

There are literally hundreds of possible combinations and scenarios, which can seem overwhelming, but this is why I've stressed the need for knowledge and the use of common sense. If we are knowledgeable about the many factors discussed, utilize our powers of observation to figure out travel patterns and other relevant "need-to-knows" and use common sense to apply logical strategies and tactics, then we have done our best. No one has a lock on how to kill every buck he goes after (at least not legally), or even the majority of them, for that matter. The subjective task of determining when to use which tactic or combination of tactics is learned best by experience. We will surely make mistakes, but we learn best by doing. Experience only makes us better at the game!

WRAPPING IT UP

Chapter 23

Concluding Thoughts

A S I SIT IN MY STUDIO/OFFICE LOOKING OVER immense shelves of
books, I scan the titles of hundreds of books written over the
last 100 years about whitetails and whitetail hunting. I'm personally
acquainted with many of the authors and familiar with the content of
most of the books. It does not come as any surprise to me that each
book is a reflection of the author. Each book is, after all, primarily
one man's (or woman's) opinion in written form.

It is quite interesting how well the subject matter and style of
each book match the personalities and interest of the authors. Mike
Biggs, for example, is a top-rate wildlife photographer and has
recently released a spectacular pictorial coffee-table book fashioned
from a photographer's perspective. Several biologists, such as
Murphy Ray, Al Brothers and James Kroll, have authored books primarily dealing with whitetail management and biology. Other writers
have covered the gamut on everything from archery hunting, record
books, general deer hunting, etc., and in each case, the author's personality, interest and specialty come shining through.

I'm not suggesting that any of these books are right or wrong,
good or bad — simply that they are an extension of their authors.
This is a revelation for me, I suppose, because this is my first book
and the first time I've looked at my own body of work relative to
other books. Over the last 15 years, I've written enough material for

The author took this 171-point typical "book" buck in Alberta while hunting with Kirk Sharp. The author had hunted the big 9-pointer for two weeks the previous season without ever seeing him. Then, on the first day of the following season, he jumped the buck from his bed and shot him on the run, pointing out that hunting where you know a big buck lives and dogged determination make a winning combination. Photo by Kirk Sharp.

10 books, but it's all been published in magazines, mostly *North American WHITETAIL,* as articles and "segments of information."

This book is my own mirror of self-analysis and causes me to reflect back on more than 30 years of whitetail hunting. How and why have I come to my own perspective of big buck hunting? The answer to that question is not so obvious to me. Yet, like the authors of the other books, the words and content of this book represent me and my philosophies, even though I had not previously viewed them in such an objective perspective.

In the final analysis, I realize I've been obsessed with nearly every facet of big bucks since I was a kid. For as long as I can remember, the uniqueness and beauty of big racks have held a special fascination for me. Each is a one-of-a-kind work of art created by mother nature. There are no two exactly alike in the world! They have an ageless, enduring quality that transcends time back to another point in history when some lucky hunter had his moment of glory.

Somewhere along the line, I concluded that if I was ever going to kill a buck as big as some of the giants I had mounted throughout my taxidermy years and had seen firsthand, I would first need to locate such a buck then spend the time on him. This perspective spawned an extensive and on-going learning curve aimed at being more successful on the really big ones. I gradually fell in love with the excitement and romance of hunting individual big bucks.

The whole process may begin with rumors of a "giant" seen crossing the road "down near Black Water Slough." The seed has been planted and the plot begins. A giant shed is found by a local farmer confirming that he does in fact exist. The plot thickens as giant rubs are found and his travel pattern is slowly unravelled. Hunting season finally arrives, and the drama builds ever faster as you "know" you have been near him sometime during the day. At the fresh scrapes and big rubs, you could even smell him. His track is unmistakable. But, he's smart and streetwise. When you make a move, he counters with his own maneuver. Then, aided by fresh snow, you get even closer, actually getting a glimpse of him. But, he was "lucky" and disappeared without a shot. The days pass and you give it your best shot, but he seems to have an uncanny ability of being "lucky" at the right times. Finally, the season ends — you don't get him. Still, you keep track of him during the off-season. There's always next year.

Occasionally, however, you will win, and when you do, success is ever so sweet! And just as the glow of success begins to dim, you hear about a monster non-typical seen near "Pothole Lake." It begins all over again.

I spend a lot of time in the woods and shoot very few bucks. For me, it's the love of the outdoors and the hunt that's most important. Don't get the wrong idea — I like to win the game once in a while and fortunately do so. Like the many different authors of books, each deer hunter carries his own motivations and personality into the woods. There is no one proper perspective so long as we have fun and derive what we want from the sport.

The "Hole-in-the-Horn" buck, discovered and made public by the author, is undoubtedly the most famous whitetail in the world. He was found dead along the railroad tracks near Kent, Ohio in 1942. He's ranked as the No. 2 non-typical in the world at 328 2/8 points. He is huge in every dimension. Even when the whereabouts of a giant like this is known, you can bet he's still going to be extremely tough to kill. Hopefully, some of the principles discussed in this book can help swing the odds of success your way. Photo by author.

In this insane world, whitetail hunting remains a common denominator where most of us can find refuge. It's a safe haven where the head is cleared and emotions untwisted. Fathers share a tradition and special times with their son. Friends gather for their annual hunt (or social) and are bonded in friendship in a way that nothing else can do. The smell of fall and the brilliant color change stir a near-religious emotion. It's a time when things are put right in the world.